Astrid de Sartiges

handpainting porcelain

Photography
Richard Boutin

Watson-Guptill Publications/New York

Acknowledgments

Astrid de Sartiges would like to thank all those who helped in the production of this book, with particular thanks to: Isabelle Jendron, Philippe Pierrelée, Valérie Tognali and Sherry Aldis at Editions du Chêne, Yvan Franusic and the house of Céradel.

Florence Le Maux and Richard Boutin would like to thank Anne and Patrick Robbé and the following companies: the house of Christofle, Habitat, Le Jacquard français, Point à la ligne and the House of Alexandre Dumas.

Florence Brutton would like to thank porcelain painter Gigi Branch for her invaluable insights into china painting.

Editor: Valérie Tognali
Design: Sabine Houplain
Layout: Florence Le Maux
Translation: Florence Brutton

Published in 2001 by Watson-Guptill Publications,
 a division of BPI Communications, Inc.
770 Broadway, New York, NY 10003.
www.watsonguptill.com

First published in France in 2000 by Éditions du Chêne, Hachette Livre

Copyright © Éditions du Chêne, Hachette Livre 2000
Photographs copyright © Richard Boutin

Library of Congress Cataloging-in-Publication Data
de Sartiges, Astrid.
    Handpainting porcelain/by Astrid de Sartiges; photography by Richard Boutin.
        p. cm.
    Includes index.
    ISBN 0-8230-2182-3
        1. Pottery craft. 2. China painting—Technique. 3. Ceramic tableware. I. Boutin, Richard.
II. Title.
TT920.D39   2001
738.1'5-dc21   2001-017892
                                                    CIP

Printed in France

1 2 3 4 5 6 7 8 9/09 08 07 06 05 04 03 02 01

Contents

INTRODUCTION

I have always loved drawing and sketching but porcelain painting was something I came across quite by chance. It all began one year in Switzerland when I signed up for an introductory course. That first day was a revelation. My teachers were experienced professionals, very much in the Nyon style and committed to perfection. I was immediately seduced.

Thanks to my teachers, I became schooled in the classic arts of porcelain painting and learned techniques developed over centuries by the great masters of this art.

Since then, guided by my imagination, I have developed a rather more personal style that incorporates both the old and the new depending on what inspires me. This book presents the fruits of my evolution as a porcelain painter. It contains a range of themes and patterns that I hope will inspire you to become more adventurous with your own designs.

I have tried to describe certain essential techniques that will add to the pleasure and fun of porcelain painting. These techniques are quite straightforward and will enable you to master such essential effects as translucency and texture; to accentuate folds in fabric; to recreate the velvetiness of fruit; and to design beautifully geometric buildings.

The motifs in this book can be used with other mediums and surfaces, including oven-set or air-dry ceramic and glass paints on china, earthenware, and glass, and acrylics on wood. Try anything, experiment as much as you can and use the ideas and practical advice given here as a springboard for your own creativity.

Just a note before you begin. The oils, essences and media needed to mix the paints are not included in the list of materials specified for each design, but can be found in Practical Tips. The paints suggested are from the Schjerning range of lead-free on-glaze colors, widely available in France. Provided you are careful to use only lead-free on-glaze paints, an alternative supplier of porcelain paints will do equally well. Happy painting!

Naughty imps

THESE CHEEKY SCAMPS DELIGHTING
IN THEIR DELICIOUS LOOT ARE
SURE TO TEMPT THE APPETITE OF
EVEN THE TINIEST TODDLER!

Set consisting of soup dish, tumbler and eggcup.

Basket after the first firing

① Transfer the motifs from the drawings on pp. 97-98 onto the soup dish, tumbler and eggcup. Paint the motifs one color at a time. For the figures on the plate and tumbler, start by painting the hair dark Albert yellow and the skin color of the face rose, adding the features after the first firing. Paint clothing and shoes violet blue and light wood brown. Paint the stone in gray for flowers.

Each time you change shades, clean your brush with orange oil (see Practical Tips, p. 92).

② Paint the basket sepia brown, dabbing lightly with the fitch brush for a smooth finish. Clean and dry the fine brush and score rows of curved strokes through the fresh paint (take care to rinse and dry the brush after every stroke). Paint the wickerwork handle as a series of interlinked 's' shapes.

③ For the raspberries in the basket, pile lots of little red balls one on top of the other. Paint the raspberries iron red and the grass and leaves in grass green and border brown (see Practical Tips on p. 95). The pieces are now ready for the first firing ①.

④ Darken the motifs. Sharpen outlines and folds in clothing. Paint the features black and the cheekbones pompadour red. When dry, add a touch of red over the black line of the nose. Darken the baskets by adding dashes of border brown. The pieces are now ready for the second firing ②.

9

Apples, caterpillars and seeds

Caterpillars or butterflies? Whichever you choose, these are ideal motifs to decorate a gift for a newborn baby. For that personal touch, add the baby's name and date of birth.

Soup dish, tumbler and eggcup set.

Soup dish
with whole apple motif

① Transfer the motifs from the drawings on p. 98 onto the dish. With rapid brushstrokes, paint the right side of the apple yellow green and the left side Albert yellow using the medium brush.

Use the sponge to dab the yellow over about a quarter of the apple on the left. With the other end of the sponge, dab the green over the rest of the apple.

② Quickly wipe around the edges of the apple using a lightly moistened cotton swab (or mask off the edges beforehand with masking fluid to prevent the color from running).

③ Use the rubber tip to remove any green paint from around the base of the stalk. Leave to dry, then paint the stalk chestnut brown. The caterpillar is made up of a series of little circles, in dark rich blue, one on top of the other, with tufts of very fine, black hairs. The pieces are now ready for the first firing ①.

④ Apply a thicker layer of color to intensify the green on the right and the yellow on the left. Dab and wipe. Define the base of the stalk in green mixed with a touch of black, and darken the color around it to suggest the hollow around the stalk. Paint over the stalk in chocolate brown. Paint the head of the caterpillar sepia brown and the legs black.

YOU WILL NEED
– Long-haired medium brush
– Long-haired fine brush
– Cotton swab or masking fluid
– Sponge
– Rubber tip
– # 8 fitch brush

PAINTS
– Motifs: Albert yellow, yellow green, chestnut brown, sepia brown, dark rich blue, ivory black, chocolate brown, ivory yellow and yellow citrus
– Rims and bands: Delft blue and pearl gray groundlay

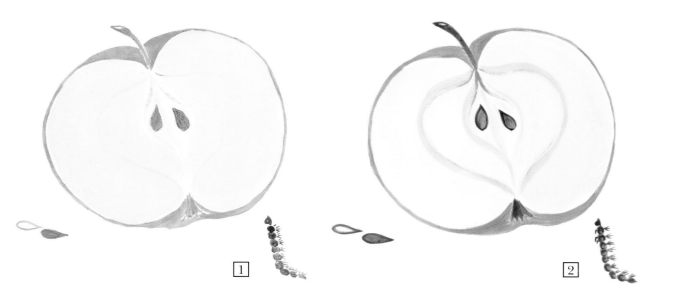

5 Paint the rim of the plate in Delft blue and pearl gray groundlay, dabbing on the color unevenly with both sides of the sponge to create a cloudy finish. The pieces are now ready for the second firing ▢.

Tumbler
with half-apple motif

1 Using the medium brush, paint the inside of the apple ivory yellow, dabbing with the fitch brush to obtain even coverage. Next, dip the fine brush in sepia and outline a large heart around the seeds. Paint the seeds, the stalk and the stem chocolate brown. Finally, paint the edges of the apple in green. The tumbler is now ready for the first firing ▢.

2 Deepen the color of the skin, the stalk and the seeds and use yellow citrus to highlight the sepia heart around the seeds. The tumbler is now ready for the second firing ▢.

3 Paint over the apple motif with masking fluid then use strips of masking tape to mark off the horizontal bands around the tumbler. Paint the bands in Delft blue and pearl gray groundlay, dabbing on the color with both sides of the sponge as for the rim of the soup dish. Fire the tumbler once again to cure the paint on the bands.

Eggcup
with seeds and caterpillars pattern

Paint seeds and caterpillars randomly over the eggcup. Paint the rim and top of the eggcup in Delft blue and pearl gray groundlay, dabbing on the color with the sponge.

Soup dish
with butterfly on branch motif

①　Transfer the motifs from p. 99. Paint the body of the butterfly black and the wings in light Albert yellow, working from the outside in. Gently stipple the wings with the fitch brush. With a single curved stroke, paint the stem of the branch first, followed by the pine needles, in grass green. Paint each one separately, pressing the brush down near the stem and moving it outwards. Paint one needle over the other where they cross. The dish is now ready for the first firing ①.

②　Cover the body of the butterfly with fine black hairs to make it darker. Paint the outline of the wings and the tapering symmetrical stripes in ivory black, then add a few red spots. Use dark prairie green mixed with a touch of black to darken one edge of the pine needles. Paint the rim of the plate in Delft blue and pearl gray groundlay, as for

the soup dish with the whole-apple motif. The dish is now ready for the second firing ②.

Tumbler
with three butterflies pattern

①　Arrange the butterflies randomly and paint as for the soup dish. Use royal blue for the marks on the wings.

②　After the second firing, paint over the butterflies with masking fluid and use masking tape to mark off the wide vertical bands.

③　Using both sides of the sponge, dab the bands unevenly with the two background colors to create a cloudy, blurred effect. Fire the tumbler once again to cure the paint on the bands.

Tumbler motifs (second firing)

YOU WILL NEED
– Long-haired fine brush
– #4 or #6 fitch brush
– Masking fluid (or resist)
– Masking tape
– Sponge

PAINTS
– Motifs: light Albert yellow, iron red, ivory black, grass green, yellow citrus, royal blue and dark prairie green
– Background: Delft blue and pearl gray groundlay

Soup dish motif

1

2

Bonbons
& Candy canes

This charming doll's house coffee set is a gift to delight children of any age — a romantic young girl or an adult with a passion for miniatures.

Set consisting of tray, three plates, two cups and saucers, coffeepot, milk jug and sugar bowl.

① Transfer the candy from the drawings on p. 97 onto the different pieces of the coffee set, choosing an appropriately sized motif for each object. Using the fine brush, start by painting the bright, irregular stripes around the middle of the candy, in light Albert yellow or pompadour red; paint the between and around them in pearl gray.

② Next, paint the gray twists of wrapping paper at each end of the candy. Emphasize the twisted shape by scoring an 's' with the rubber tip. Paint the candy canes as a series of red or light wood brown and egg yellow rope-like twists. The pieces are now ready for the first firing ☐.

③ Using gray mixed with a dash of black, darken the outline of the candy and emphasize the

twists in the wrapping paper. Intensify the existing colors of the candy canes stressing the twists.

④ For the tray, use masking tape to mark off the square round the motifs. Darken the candy as before and use the sponge to apply the yellow citrus background. Be careful not to touch the motifs. Leave to dry. Meanwhile, paint the handles. The pieces are now ready for the second firing ☐.

⑤ Paint over the candy, handles and yellow rim of the plate with masking fluid. As before, use the sponge to apply yellow green or yellow citrus groundlay to the different pieces. Leave to dry, then remove the masking fluid and scrape off any splatters around the motifs. Fire once again to cure the groundlay.

YOU WILL NEED
– Long-haired fine brush
– Masking fluid (resist)
– Masking tape
– Sponge (to apply groundlay)
– Rubber tip
– Scraper

PAINTS
– Motifs: yellow citrus, egg yellow, pearl gray, pompadour red, light-wood brown, light Albert yellow and black
– Background: yellow green or yellow citrus groundlay

Miniature coffee set motifs (second firing)

19

Spring is
in the air

BOLDLY COLORED FLOWERS ON
A FRESH, GREEN BACKGROUND
GIVE THESE COFFEE CUPS A
LIVELY, SPRING-LIKE APPEARANCE.

YOU WILL NEED
– Long-haired fine brush
– Long-haired medium brush
– #4 or #6 fitch brush
– Masking fluid (or resist)
– Rubber tip
– Sponge (to apply groundlay)
– Chinagraph pencil

PAINTS
Hibiscus
– Motif: grass green (light and dark), brown red ①; black ②.
– Background: yellow green groundlay

Set of six coffee cups and saucers
Decorate each cup and saucer with one of six different flower motifs (hibiscus, pansies, roses, tulips, magnolia and dandelions), including leaves and buds.

Hibiscus cup and saucer

① Transfer the flower from p. 100 onto the front of the cup and the bud and leaf onto the back. With a chinagraph pencil, draw the small bud freehand onto the inside of the cup (below the rim). Mix the colors (both shades of green and the red) on the same palette so that you can graduate the green on the leaves.

② Using the medium brush, paint the flower one petal at a time, leaving a slight gap between each one. Shade the petals, graduating the red on the outside of the flower from dark to light nearer the center; leave a white space in the middle. Use the fitch brush to stipple the color lightly and evenly over each petal. Wipe around and redefine each petal with the rubber tip.

③ Paint the stem and the leaves green. Paint the red buds at the back of the cup and on the inside, below the rim. The cup is now ready for the first firing ①.

④ Intensify the color of the flower, one petal at a time, in the same red as before. Use grass green mixed with a dash of black to darken the leaves, emphasizing the fold in the leaf on the right and highlighting the leaf on the left. The cup is now ready for the second firing ②.

⑤ Resist out the flower, leaves, bud and handle with masking fluid and leave to dry completely. Now use the sponge to apply yellow green groundlay over the cup and saucer. When dry, remove the masking fluid and fire to cure the groundlay.

⑥ For the saucer, use the chinagraph pencil to trace the garland from the drawing on p. 100 and transfer it onto the green background. Paint in green mixed with a dash of black, as a continuous ring of 'tear drop' shapes. Press the brush down, curve the stroke towards you and lif off to create a pointed tip. Repeat until you have a complete garland. Use the same color for the tapering stripe through the center of the handle. Fire once again.

Create the other flowers in the same way. Always remember to draw every brushstroke towards you, turning the cup or saucer as you work.

Motif on the front of the cup

1

2

Cup handle

Garland around the saucer

1

Motif at the back of the cup

2

1   2

Motif on the inside of the cup

1

Motif on the front of the cup

2

PAINTS
Pansy

– Motif: light Albert yellow, grass green (light and dark) 1; ruby purple, canary yellow, black 2.

– Background: yellow green groundlay

1

Motif at the back of the cup

2

1

2

Motif on the inside of the cup

Motif on the front of the cup

1

2

Motif on the inside of the cup

1   2

1   2

Motif at the back of the cup

1   2

PAINTS

Rose

– Motif: purple, grass green (light and dark) 1; golden ruby and black 2.
– Background: yellow green groundlay

Motif on the front of the cup

1   2

PAINTS

Tulip

– Motif: brown red, grass green (light and dark) 1; black 2.
– Background: yellow green groundlay

Motif on the inside of the cup

1   2

Motif at the back of the cup

1   2

Motif on the front of the cup

Motif on the inside of the cup

Motif at the back of the cup

PAINTS
Magnolia

– Motif: purple, grass green (light and dark) ☐1; golden ruby and black ☐2.

– Background: yellow green groundlay

Motif on the front of the cup

PAINTS
Dandelion

– Motif: light Albert yellow, grass green (light and dark) ☐1; canary yellow and black ☐2.

– Background: yellow green groundlay

Motif on the inside of the cup

Motif at the back of the cup

YOU WILL NEED
– Long-haired medium brush
– Long-haired fine brush
– #6 fitch brush
– Masking fluid (or resist)
– Masking tape
– Rubber tip
– Sponge (to apply groundlay)
– Flux

PAINTS
– Motifs: rose purple and grass green ①; potpourri and black ②
– Alternating colors for background and external borders: potpourri and yellow green groundlay

Hors-d'Œuvres dish

Set consisting of two matching hors-d'œuvres dishes with backgrounds and external borders in alternating colors.

Hors-d'œuvres dish
with tulip motif

① Transfer the three tulips from p. 102 and cut into three separate tracings. Place a piece of graphite paper over the dishes and tape the tracings into position. If you want, you can also decorate the front of the dish.

② With broad, rounded brushstrokes, paint the open and half-open tulips purple. The arrows show the directions of the brushstrokes. Remember to draw the brush towards you. Start with the central petal, working from the widest to the narrowest point. Stipple each petal individually with the fitch brush to obtain a smooth finish.

③ Use the rubber tip to score a delicate delineation between the petals. Next, still in the direction of the arrows and drawing every stroke towards you, paint the leaves and stems green. Because the tulip bud is such a small area of purple, paint the leaf first and add the bud once the green has dried. The dish is now ready for the first firing ①.

④ Use green mixed with a dash of black to darken the stem at the base of the petals and the leaves. Paint lines on the petals in potpourri in the direction of the arrows. Press the brush down and curve the stroke towards you. The dish is now ready for the second firing ②.

⑤ Resist out the three flowers with masking fluid and leave to dry. Paint the background in groundlay mixed with a dash of flux to ensure a shiny finish. Leave to dry. Use two parallel strips of masking tape to mark off a border 1/4"(0.5 cm) wide around the outside edge of the dish just below the rim. Paint in green for the dish with the purple background and vice versa. Wipe neatly and fire to cure the groundlay and borders.

Create the rose motif in the same way.

1

2

1

2

Ring a ring of roses...

These delightful coffee
cups in crisp, bright tones
breathe new life into an
old-fashioned motif and add
sparkle to any interior.

Set of six coffee cups and saucers.

YOU WILL NEED

– Long-haired fine brush
– Masking fluid (or resist)
– Rubber tip
– Sponge (to apply groundlay)
– Chinagraph pencil
– Pointed instrument and tweezers (for removing resist)
– Scraper (for retouching)

PAINTS

– Petals: yellow red, yellow citrus, rose purple, light Albert yellow pearl gray and potpourri
– Centers: light Albert yellow, Albert yellow, chestnut brown
– Leaves: grass green and black
– Background: yellow green, rich blue, Albert yellow deep, yellow red, potpourri and pearl gray groundlay

① Using the chinagraph pencil, draw a line around the cup and saucer, about 1 1/4" (3 cm) from the rim. Transfer the garlands from the drawings on p. 104 onto this line. Alternatively, draw them freehand, starting with the flowers and adding the leaves and rose buds in the spaces between.

② Paint the flowers one petal at a time leaving the center white. Next paint the leaves and with the paint still fresh, use the rubber tip (see Practical Tips, p. 93) to create a serrated edge. Remember to draw the tip towards you for precision.

③ Paint the leaves of the rosebuds green but wait until dry before you paint the rosebud itself. Once the petals have dried, add spots of chestnut brown around the white centers of the roses. The pieces are now ready for the first firing ①.

④ Shade part of the petals in potpourri and part of the leaves with green mixed with a dash of black. Paint the white centers yellow and intensify the brown spots around the centers. The pieces are now ready for the second firing ②.

⑤ For the colored borders, start by resisting out the top of the garlands and the cup handle with masking fluid and leave to dry. Apply groundlay with the sponge and when completely dry, carefully remove the masking fluid with a pointed instrument and tweezers. Use the scraper for any retouching. Fire once again to cure the groundlay.

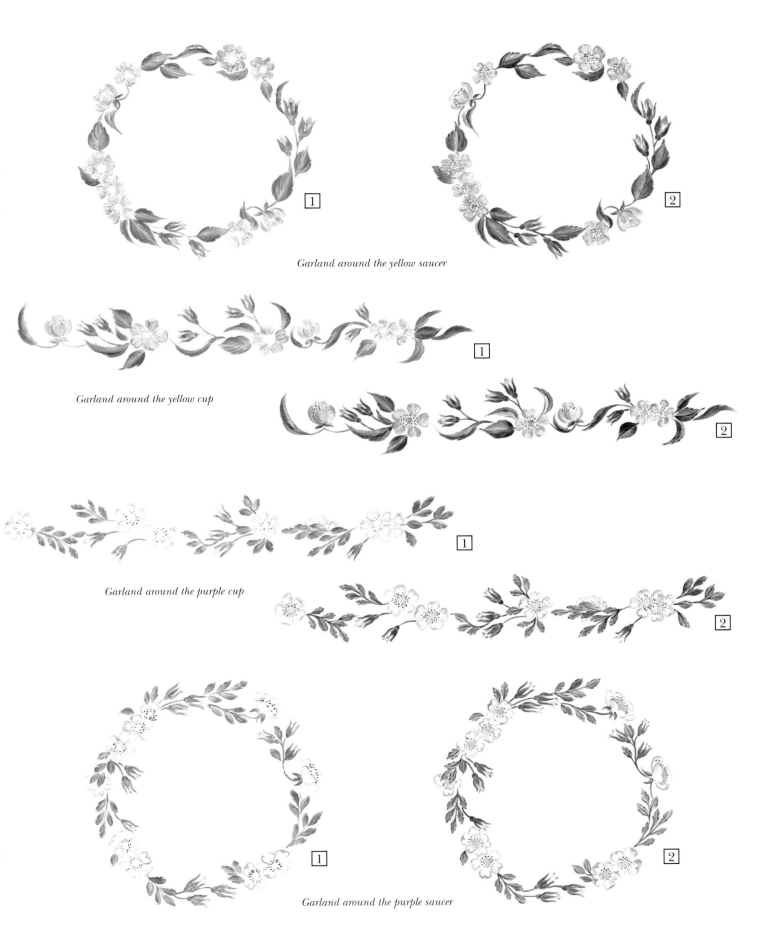

Garland around the yellow saucer

Garland around the yellow cup

Garland around the purple cup

Garland around the purple saucer

roses,
roses
everywhere...

YELLOW, PINK, WHITE AND PURPLE
ROSES ADD SUBTLE CHARM TO THIS SET
OF FOUR SCALLOPED HORS-D'OEUVRES
DISHES IN SHADES OF EMERALD.

1

Motif at the front of the dish
(first firing)

2

Motifs at the back
of the dish (second firing)

YOU WILL NEED

– Long-haired fine brush
– Short-haired fine brush
– Sponge (to apply groundlay)
– Masking fluid (or resist)
– Rubber tip
– Pointed instrument
  (to remove resist)

PAINTS

– Light Albert yellow, purple,
  pearl gray, rose purple, grass
  green and chestnut brown 1;
  dark Albert yellow, potpourri
  gray and black 2.
– Background: Meissen green
  groundlay
– Relief dots: white relief,
  Meissen green and general
  purpose medium (or fat oil)

① Transfer the motifs from the drawings on p.106 onto the front and back of each dish. Paint the central petal first, working upwards from the base. Curve the brushstroke towards you in the direction indicated by the arrows. Next, still drawing the stroke towards you, paint the leaves and score little notches in the fresh paint with the rubber tip to create a serrated edge.

Paint the thorns on the stems with the fine brush. Use the same technique for the roses on both sides of the dish. The dish is now ready for the first firing 1.

② Darken part of the leaves with green mixed with a dash of black, and intensify parts of the petals. You are now ready to add the green dots (around the central rose at the front, and in the vertical lines and white sections at the back). To make the dots, mix white relief with general purpose medium (or fat oil) and Meissen green. Aim for a thick mixture with the smooth consistency of mastic that does not spread when dropped onto a ceramic tile. Add more white relief if necessary and when the mixture is thick enough, use the short-haired fine brush to add the dots at the front and back of the dish and leave to dry completely. The dish is now ready for the second firing 2.

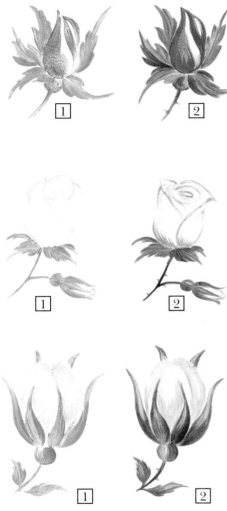

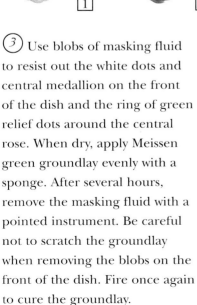

③ Use blobs of masking fluid
to resist out the white dots and
central medallion on the front
of the dish and the ring of green
relief dots around the central
rose. When dry, apply Meissen
green groundlay evenly with a
sponge. After several hours,
remove the masking fluid with a
pointed instrument. Be careful
not to scratch the groundlay
when removing the blobs on the
front of the dish. Fire once again
to cure the groundlay.

④ Turn the dish over and use
masking fluid to resist out the
flowers and vertical lines of relief
dots on the back. Apply Meissen
green groundlay to the areas
round the motifs, leave to dry
completely and remove the
masking fluid. Fire once again
to cure the groundlay at the
back of the dish.

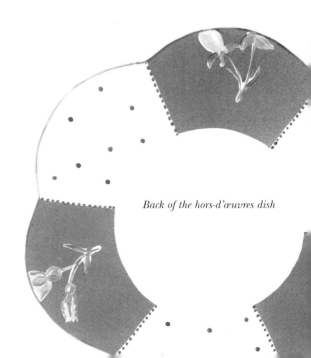

Back of the hors-d'œuvres dish

view from the Balcony

BE THE ARCHITECT OF YOUR
DESIRES: PAINT YOUR OWN DREAM
APARTMENT, BRICK BY BRICK,
COMPLETE WITH WROUGHT IRON
BALCONY AND — WHAT CITY
STREET WOULD BE COMPLETE
WITHOUT THEM — PASSERSBY
AND THEIR DOGS.

Set of six cups and saucers.

YOU WILL NEED

– Long-haired fine brush
– #6 fitch brush
– Cut liner
– Mapping pen
– Pen oil (or liquid sweetener)
– Chinagraph pencil
– Lining tool
– Masking fluid (or resist)
– Rubber tip
– Scraper
– Short ruler
– Banding wheel (or masking tape)
– Sponges

Cups

(1) Carefully transfer the building façade from the drawings on p. 108 onto the cup. Mix the pearl gray with liquid sweetener or pen oil (see Practical Tips, p. 93) and draw around the outline with the mapping pen. When dry, make sure that the finish does not smudge when rubbed.

(2) Next paint the insides of the windows black, stippling with the fitch brush to obtain a smooth finish. When completely dry (several hours later) use the ruler and scraper to create the windowpanes. Place the ruler lengthwise down the middle of each window and score a thick, vertical white line in the black paint (make sure the ruler stays firmly in place). Next, place the ruler crosswise and score the horizontal lines. Wipe clean. Paint the stonework and columns sepia brown, the bricks red, the doorframes border brown and the balconies ivory black. The cup is now ready for the first firing ①.

(3) At this stage, you can more easily darken the bricks and stonework, highlight the outlines of the doors and windows and redefine the balconies in black. The cup is now ready for the second firing ②.

(4) Resist out the façades and cup handles with masking fluid. Apply egg yellow or light wood brown groundlay with the sponge

and when dry, remove the resist and wipe neatly. Fire once again to cure the groundlay.

⑤ Transfer the figures and pigeons (also from the drawings on p. 108) onto the groundlay on the cup. Paint the figures black and, while the paint is still fresh, use the rubber tip to sharpen the images and accentuate the movement of the arms, knees, etc. Fire once again to cure the black.

Saucers

① Using the lining tool and chinagraph pencil, draw two parallel pencil lines, one about 1/16" (0.2 cm) from the rim and the second about 1/2" (1.3 cm) from the rim. Next, place the saucer on the banding wheel and paint the lines black with the cut liner. If you do not have access to a banding wheel, mark off the lines with masking tape and paint with a mapping pen. Divide the balconies into even sections with single or double vertical lines. The saucer is now ready for the first firing ①.

② Transfer the balcony pattern from the drawings on p. 108 onto the saucer. Paint with a fine brush or mapping pen (remember the paint needs to be thinner for penwork). The saucer is now ready for the second firing ②.

③ Resist out the borders and centers of the saucer with masking fluid. Apply groundlay to match the background on the cup. Fire once again to cure the groundlay.

You can use the same balcony pattern to decorate a milk jug, sugar bowl, tray, etc.

PAINTS

– Motifs: iron red, sepia brown, border brown and ivory black
– Paint for penwork: pearl gray
– Backgrounds: egg yellow and light wood brown groundlay

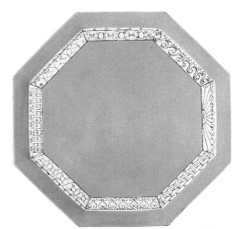

Calli*graphy*

THIS BRIGHT YELLOW COFFEE SET IS A RIOT OF RED LETTERS. FIND OUT HOW TO CREATE AN AMUSING ALPHABET OF YOUR OWN.

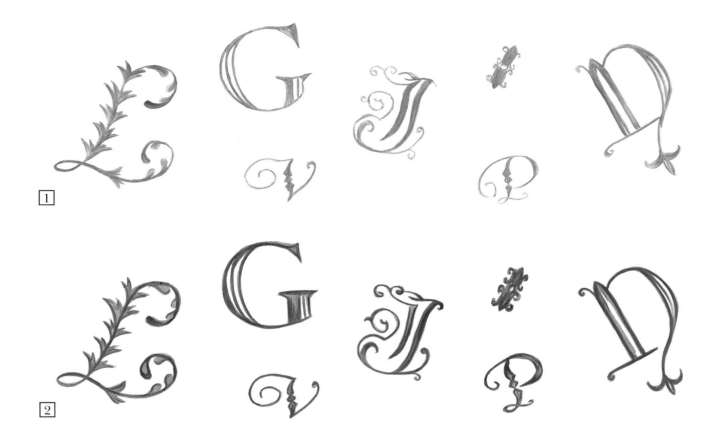

Set of six cups and saucers and cake dish.

1 Choose from the wide selection of letters on pp. 109-112, varying the size to suit the object to be decorated. Trace, and tape the tracings onto the cups and saucers so as to obtain an even distribution of small and large letters.

2 Paint with the fine brush, pressing down where the letter broadens and drawing the stroke smoothly towards you. While the paint is still fresh, sharpen the outlines with the rubber tip, or use the scraper if the paint has already dried. The pieces are now ready for the first firing ①.

3 Darken part of each letter, leaving broad, light areas to create contrast. The pieces are now ready for the second firing ②.

4 Use masking fluid to resist out the cup handle and the letters on the cup and center of the saucer. When dry, use the sponge to paint the backgrounds in yellow groundlay and fire once again.

If you prefer, you can leave the background white and add a decorative colored or gold border (see 'Gold and Platinum' in Practical Tips, p. 91).

YOU WILL NEED
– Long-haired fine brush
– Masking fluid (or resist)
– Sponge (to apply groundlay)
– Rubber tip or scraper

PAINTS
– Motifs: iron red
– Background: egg yellow groundlay

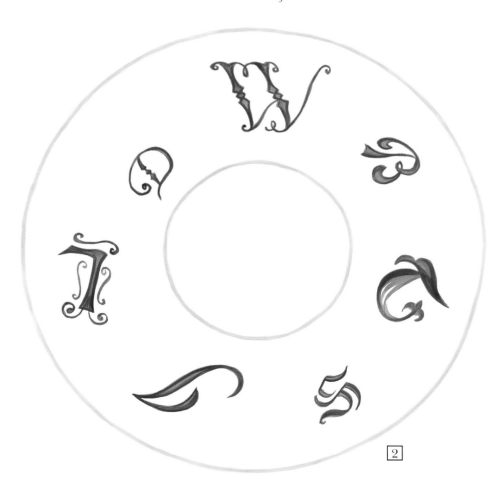

Saucer motifs

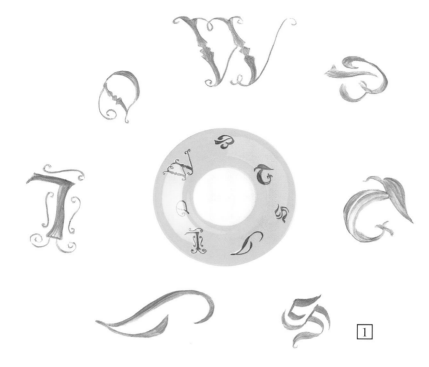

45

mountain chalet

Bring the clear air of
the mountains to your
table all year round
with these crisp,
green alpine motifs.

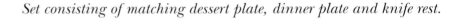

Set consisting of matching dessert plate, dinner plate and knife rest.

Y O U W I L L N E E D
– Long-haired fine brush
– Long-haired very fine brush
– Sponge (for borders)
– #4 fitch brush

P A I N T S
– Meissen green

Dessert plate

1 Position the motifs around the edge of the plate so that they are evenly spaced and transfer from the drawings on p. 113. Leave enough room for a border around the rim.

2 Using the fine brush, paint the motifs with a thin layer of green. Stipple broad areas on the cow with the fitch brush but keep well away from the head and legs to avoid the need for subsequent cleaning.

3 When the motifs are completely dry, add the colored border. Moisten the sponge with paint and dab the color all along the scalloped rim. You are aiming for an irregular effect typical of rustic, alpine pottery. The plate is now ready for the first firing ▢.

④ Go over each motif once again with the very fine brush. In particular, intensify the green of the cows to sharpen the outline of the ears, horns, tail, collar and bell. The plate is now ready for the second firing ②.

Dinner plate

Proceed as for the dessert plate but do not add the colored border – which is wider and closer to the motifs – until after the second firing.

Knife rest

Decorate with simple motifs recalling those on the plates – a

tiny flower and heart, for instance. Sponge an even border along all the edges and corners and fire.

Use 'negatives' of the same motifs to decorate a salad bowl, pepper pot, mustard pot, milk jug, etc. Transfer the motifs, resist out with masking fluid and when dry, paint all over with groundlay.

1

2

Gourds and insects

An amusing collection of
squash, butternut squash
and pumpkins with mysterious
insects buzzing attendance,
add warm autumnal
tones to a set of four
hors-d'oeuvres dishes.

1

2

Dish
with butternut squash

① Transfer the butternut squash from p. 114 onto the dish. Paint in yellow brown with the medium brush, then stipple quickly with the fitch brush before the paint dries. Rinse the medium brush in orange oil and wipe clean.

Now score a series of wavy lines down the length of the squash to bring out its naturally curved shape. Add a touch of brown green at the base of the squash and stipple to obtain a subtle blend of color. Create the stalk as a series of sepia brown 's' shapes.

② When dry, paint the insect. Start with the black body then go over the wings in ochre. Paint from the tip of the wing towards the insect's body, pressing the brush down and drawing it

– Long-haired medium brush
– Long-haired fine brush
– #8 or # 10 fitch brush
– Masking tape
– Sponge
– Orange oil

1

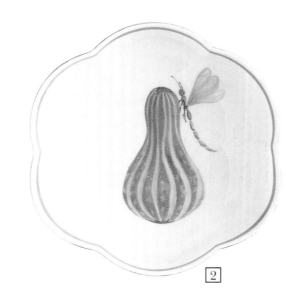

2

1

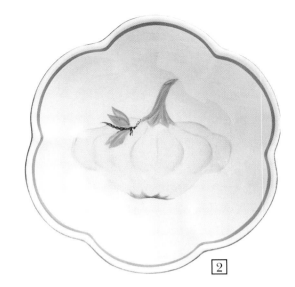

2

smoothly towards you.

Paint the legs with the fine brush. Turn the dish over and place on an old rigid table mat. Use the sponge to stipple the exterior in iron red and leave to dry. The dish is now ready for the first firing 1.

③ Deepen the color on one side of the squash, the stalk and the insect body. Accentuate the wings by adding very fine black lines. Without touching the motif, use masking tape to create a parallel border round the dish. Stick one strip of masking tape around the entire rim of the dish and a second slightly below it. Stipple the narrow space between with iron red. The dish is now ready for the second firing 2.

Create the three other dishes (with insects) in the same way.

PAINTS

– Butternut squash: yellow brown, brown green, sepia brown, ochre and black
– Green squash: grass green, yellow citrus, chestnut brown, sepia brown and black
– White squash: ivory yellow, sepia brown, light wood brown, brown green and black
– Pumpkin squash: Albert yellow, sienna, brown green, light wood brown and black
– Borders and exterior: iron red

1

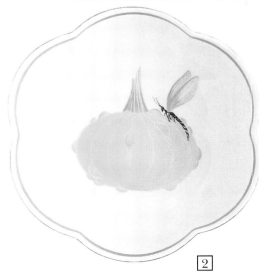

2

Seashells buried in the sand

THIS SET OF PLATES IS IDEAL

FOR LUNCH OR DINNER

BY THE SEA, OR TO RECAPTURE

THE SOUND OF THE WAVES

WHEN THE VACATION IS OVER.

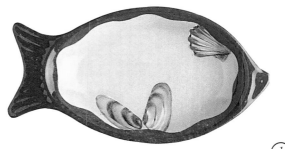

Set of two large plates and two dessert plates.

① Start with the borders, adding the seashells afterwards as if they were partly hidden in the sand. Trace the wavy outline provided on pp. 115-116 and use to make a cardboard cutout (or create your own to suit the size of plate). Make it look as wavy as possible.

② Using masking fluid, resist out the wavy edge on the inside of the plate. When dry, use the make-up brush to stipple the border round the outside edge of the plate. Leave to dry then remove the resist and sharpen the border with the scraper. Fire the plate to cure the border.

③ Mix all your colors on the same palette. Transfer the seashells from the drawings on p. 117 onto the plate. Paint them one at a time, with the medium brush, then stipple lightly with the fitch brush.

④ While the paint is still fresh, define the flutes in the scallop shells by scoring the brush through the paint to leave a delicate line. Make as many lines as necessary, wiping the brush clean every time. Use the same technique to create smaller and smaller 's' shapes on the coiled, spiral shells. The plate is now ready for the first firing ☐.

⑤ Intensify the outlines and scoops in the shells. Finally shade one side of the spiral shells and stipple with the fitch brush. The plate is now ready for the second firing ☐.

Use the seashell motifs to decorate butter dishes, hors-d'oeuvres dishes, knife rests, etc.

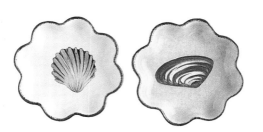

YOU WILL NEED
– Long-haired medium brush
– #4 or #6 fitch brush
– Make-up brush
– Masking fluid (or resist)
– Scraper

PAINTS
– Motifs: brown red, ivory black, violet blue, rose purple, chestnut brown, sepia brown and eye gray
– Borders: sienna groundlay

Dessert plate motifs

Variations on
a theme
of gray

MIMOSAS, PANSIES, SUNFLOWERS,

ROSES, TULIPS AND BROOM

ALL COMBINE WITH A FLOURISH

ON THIS INVITING DINNER

SERVICE IN WARM TONES OF

YELLOW, OCHRE AND GRAY.

Mimosa centerpiece for the dessert plate

Set of six large plates, six dessert plates, six side plates and matching knife rests.

YOU WILL NEED
– Long-haired medium brush
– Long-haired fine brush (for the smaller motifs on the side plates)
– Masking fluid (or resist)
– Rubber tip
– Scraper (for retouching)
– Masking tape
– Sponge

PAINTS
– Motifs: yellow citrus, grass green, dark Albert yellow, sepia brown and black
– Backgrounds: pearl gray groundlay + flux (for the dessert plates); light wood brown groundlay (for the large plates); pearl gray and light wood brown groundlay (for the side plates)

Dessert plate
with bouquet of mimosa

① Transfer the bouquet from p. 119 onto the center of the plate. Start by painting the flowers yellow citrus, overlaying them in places (see Practical Tips, p. 96). Use light brush strokes to ensure a delicate finish before firing.

② Paint the leaves (see Practical Tips, p. 95) crossing one over the other where shown. The plate is now ready for the first firing ①.

③ With a curved stroke, shade half the flower in dark Albert yellow, and half the leaves in green mixed with a dash of black. Use the shading to delineate flowers that are overlaid or leaves that are crossed.

④ Add touches of sepia brown to the flowers to give them a velvety appearance. Join them together with delicately curved strokes to form the stems. The plate is now ready for the second firing ②.

⑤ Resist out the motif with masking fluid. When dry, use a sponge to cover the rest of the plate in pearl gray groundlay mixed with a drop of flux to ensure a shiny finish. Fire once again to cure the groundlay.

Large plate
with mimosa border

① Transfer the motifs from the drawings on p. 118 onto the edge of the plate. Paint as for the dessert plate.

② After the second firing, resist out the motifs with masking fluid and mask off the inner edge of the plate with masking tape. Paint the edge of the plate in light wood brown groundlay and fire again.

Side plate
with garland of mimosa

① Draw the garland freehand, or transfer from the drawings on p. 118. It should straddle the inside edge of the plate.

② Paint as before but using a brush with a finer point. Delineate the flowers and leaves with the rubber tip. Paint the background as before in pearl gray groundlay.

Knife rest

① Paint with a single motif consisting of two or three flowers and a single leaf.

② When dry, use the sponge to stipple both sides of the knife rest in light wood brown and leave to dry once again. The piece is now ready for the first firing 1.

③ Paint over the motifs with masking fluid and sponge gray groundlay onto the front and back of the knife rest, not forgetting the two ends. Leave to dry then fire once again 2.

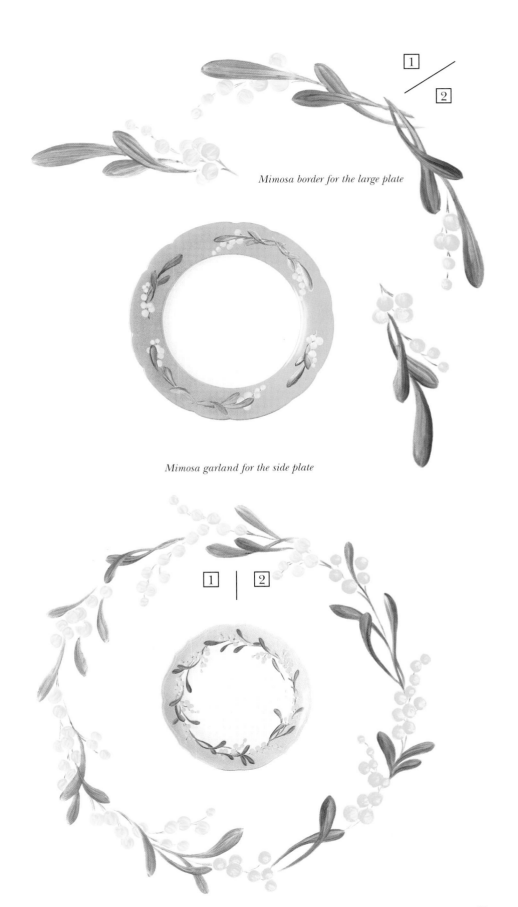

Mimosa border for the large plate

Mimosa garland for the side plate

61

Pansy centerpiece for the dessert plate

Pansy garland for the side plate

Pansy border for the large plate.

Pansy motif

Transfer from the drawings on pp. 120-121 onto the plates. Paint as for the mimosa, in the same colors, adding delicate purple lines to form the center of the flower. The leaves are broad, wavy and serrated – use the rubber tip as suggested in Practical Tips (see p. 95).

1 | 2

Sunflower garland for the side plate

1 / 2

Sunflower centerpiece for the dessert plate

1 | 2

Sunflower border for the large plate.

Tulip motif
Transfer from the drawings on pp. 126-127 onto the plates. Paint as before, in the same colors, adding spots of sepia brown to form the center of the open flower.

Rose motif
Transfer from the drawings on pp. 124-125 onto the plates. Paint as before, in the same colors, adding spots of sepia brown for the center.

Sunflower motif
Transfer from the drawings on pp. 122-123 onto the plates. Paint as before, in the same colors, adding spots of sepia brown to form the center.

Broom motif
Transfer from the drawings on pp. 128-129 onto the plates. Paint as for the mimosa.

A flurry of feathers

WISPS OF COLOR TO START YOUR
DAY. PAMPER YOURSELF IN THE
MORNING WITH THIS CHARMING
PORCELAIN SOFTLY FLUTTERING
WITH FEATHERS ...

YOU WILL NEED
– Long-haired, very fine brush
– Rubber tip
– Masking tape

PAINTS
– Feather motifs: eye gray, new
  blue, grass green, dark Albert
  yellow, sepia brown and flesh
  red (light colors [1]); black,
  carmine blue light, chestnut
  brown and brown red [2].
– Geometric motifs: sienna and
  chestnut brown
– Borders: chocolate brown

Set consisting of a cup and saucer with matching cake dish.

(1) Transfer each feather from the drawings on p. 130 onto the pieces of the set. Paint in the lighter of the suggested shades so that you can add contrast after the first firing. Start with the gray of the central spine, emphasizing the curve in the feather.

(2) Create the wispy gray down at the base of the feather with the very fine brush. Using your lightest touch, trace a line from the feather's spine to the tip of each wisp. Try to apply no pressure at all and use only the tip of the brush. (As always, to ensure precision, draw each stroke towards you.)

(3) Paint the rest of the feather as for the down, using slightly smoother but equally light brushstrokes. The featheriness of the motifs depends upon this delicate brushwork. Use only the tip of the brush with your lightest possible touch.

(4) Paint the geometric Chinese motifs that give weight to an otherwise airy design. Use the rubber tip to add the final touch to the feathers, separating the tufts in places. The pieces are now ready for the first firing [1].

(5) Darken the central spine by adding a touch of black along part of its length. Darken the gray wisps without making the brushwork heavier. Intensify the different colors of the feathers and draw a dark brown outline around the geometric motifs. The pieces are now ready for the second firing [2].

(6) Mask off the edges of the cup, saucer and dish and paint the border around the rim. Fire once again.

You can use the same motifs, with different colored borders, to decorate a tray, milk jug, sugar bowl, etc.

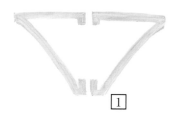

1

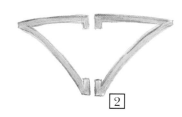

2

1

2

1

2

1

2

1

2

...ïorriMMirror...

These coffee cups and saucers reflect a glittering array of motifs — mirrors, lamps, frames, flasks, candlesticks and silver goblets — in a handsome platinum finish.

Set of six coffee cups and saucers.

YOU WILL NEED
– Long-haired fine brush
– Short-haired fine brush
   (to apply the platinum)
– Masking tape
– Platinum thinner
– Sponge
– Scraper
– Rubber tip
– Ceramic mixing tile
– Orange stick (to stir platinum)

PAINTS
– Motifs: brilliant platinum, Albert
   yellow deep, grass green, Sienna,
   iron red, chestnut brown, ivory
   black and gray for flowers
– Backgrounds: yellow citrus,
   violet blue and yellow green
   groundlay

① Divide the cups into eight vertical sections. Use masking tape to mask off the four colored sections, leaving the central handle section white (see the drawings on p. 136). Next, use the tape to mask out a straight border 1/4" (0.5 cm) wide along the rim of the cup and saucer. Use the sponge to paint the backgrounds on the saucers and the four colored sections. When dry, remove the tape and use the scraper to clean off any splatters. Fire to cure the backgrounds ▯.

② Transfer the motifs from the drawings on p. 136 onto the white sections of the cups. Using the illustrations as a guide, paint the colored parts of the motifs (candles, shades, flowers, etc.) and leave to dry. Next, stir the platinum with an orange stick and place a drop of paint on a ceramic mixing

tile. Fill the short-haired brush and apply a thin, even layer of platinum to the silver areas of the motifs using platinum thinner as needed (see 'Gold and Platinum' in Practical Tips, p. 91). Use the long-haired brush to paint the ornamental moldings.

③ Now create a platinum ring of dashes around the white rim of the cups and saucers, skirting the colored sections. The pieces are now ready for the second firing ▯. Platinum should be fired at 1470˚F (800˚C) when applied to white porcelain and needs no polishing after firing.

④ Without touching the platinum areas, darken the colored parts of the motifs to create contrast. The pieces are now ready for a third firing.

s t a r r y,

Starry, night...

RECREATE THE MAGIC OF
CHRISTMAS AND WARM, FESTIVE
NIGHTS AROUND THE DINNER
TABLE WITH THIS SET OF PLATES
WREATHED IN HOLLY AND
TWINKLING WITH GOLD AND
SILVER STARS.

Holly centerpiece for the starter plate

Set consisting of a starter plate, large plate, side-plate and matching knife rest.

YOU WILL NEED

– Long-haired medium brush
– Long-haired fine brush
– Two short-haired very fine brushes (to apply the gold and platinum)
– #4 or #6 fitch brush
– Rubber tip
– Masking fluid (or resist)
– Masking tape
– Sponge
– Scraper

PAINTS

Starter plate with holly centerpiece
– Motifs: grass green, iron red and black
– Background: pearl gray groundlay + flux
Large plate with holly border
– Motifs: as above
– Background: Delft blue groundlay + flux
Side plate with stars
– Motifs: gold or platinum

Starter plate
with holly centerpiece

1 Transfer the holly centerpiece from the drawings on p. 131 onto the plate. Paint the leaves one at a time (see Practical Tips, p. 95) using the fitch brush first, then the tip of the fine brush to form the sharp prickly points.

2 Paint the red berries, overlaying them in places or tucking them partly under the leaves. With the paint still fresh, use the rubber tip to delineate the berries and score a central spine down the leaves. The plate is now ready for the first firing ①.

3 Darken the leaves but not the folds, which should remain light. Darken along the edges of overlaid berries to make it possible to distinguish between them. The plate is now ready for the second firing ②.

4 Resist out the motifs with masking fluid. When dry, paint the rest of the plate in pearl gray groundlay mixed with a dash of flux. Remove the masking fluid with a scraper and fire again.

Large plate
with holly border

1 Transfer the holly leaves and red berries from the drawings on p. 131 onto the plate. Paint and fire as for the starter plate.

Holly border for the large plate

② Resist out the motifs and the center of the plate. Use the sponge to paint the edge of the plate with Delft blue groundlay mixed with a dash of flux. When dry, remove the masking fluid, taking care not to scratch the blue. Fire once again to cure the groundlay.

Side plate
with stars

① Using masking fluid, paint star shapes around the border of the plate and mask out the center with masking tape. Sponge the edge of the plate with Delft blue groundlay mixed with a dash of flux and leave to dry completely.

② Use the scraper to remove the resist star shapes (taking care not to scratch the blue groundlay) and to sharpen the outlines of the stars. The plate is now ready for the first firing ①.

③ Using a separate very fine brush for each color, paint the stars in gold or platinum. Fire at 1470°F (800°C), the recommended temperature for precious metals applied to white backgrounds (see 'Gold and Platinum' in Practical Tips, p. 91). Neither the gold nor the platinum need polishing.

Matching knife rest

Paint and fire as for the side plate with stars.

A thousand and One nights

Transform your table into a gateway to the Orient: figures and landscapes straight from the Arabian nights will transport your guests to a land full of eastern promise...

YOU WILL NEED

- Long-haired fine brush
- Long-haired very fine brush
- #4 fitch brush
- Cut liner
- Masking fluid (or resist)
- Make-up brush
- Rubber tip
- Banding wheel
  (for the dessert plate)
- Sponge
- Scraper

PAINTS

Side plate with oriental figures
- Smoker: sky blue, pearl gray, brown red, sepia brown and black
- Carpet seller: Sienna, violet blue, sky blue, pearl gray, brown red, sepia brown and black
- Fruit seller: light wood brown, violet blue, sky blue, pearl gray, brown red, sepia brown and black
- Musician: Sienna, violet blue, sky blue, brown red, sepia brown and black
- Praying man: sky blue, brown red, sepia brown and black
- Painter: as for the carpet seller but omit sky blue bluish
- Background: brown red groundlay

Dinner set

Dinner set of six side plates (with oriental figures), six dessert plates (with oriental figures in richer colored robes) and six large plates (with desert landscapes). There are knife rests, candlesticks and coffee cups to match.

Side plate
The instructions are the same for each plate.

① As carefully as you can, transfer a figure from the drawings on p. 132 onto the center of the plate. Mix your paints, then paint the figure one color at a time with the fine brush. Complete each part of the drawing separately, applying lines of more intense color to accentuate movement (such as the curved back, rounded shoulder, bent knee or elbow).

② Using the fitch brush, gently stipple the lines in the picture to create a watercolor effect. At the same time, separate the different colors by leaving a thin line of white between them. Clean well around the edges of the motif before firing, using the rubber tip if the paint is still fresh, or with the scraper if the paint has dried. The plate is now ready for the first firing ①.

③ Mix the same colors as before but apply them more thickly this time. With the fine brush, revive areas of color that may have faded during firing. As before, accentuate movement and suppleness by highlighting

shoulders and knees and folds in clothing. With the very fine brush, darken the beard and eyelashes in black and the hands and feet in sepia brown. The plate is now ready for the second firing ②.

④ Draw the oriental doorway freehand, or trace from the drawings on p. 135. Transfer onto the plate so that it frames the motif, allowing parts of the motif to bleed off (see illustrations). Resist out the motif and doorway with masking fluid. When completely dry, use the make-up brush like a sponge to dab on brown red groundlay. You are aiming for an even distribution of paint with a granite-like or sandy finish.

⑤ When the background is dry, remove the masking fluid and sharpen the outline of the door with a scraper. Fire once again to cure the groundlay.

1

Smoker *Carpet seller* *Fruit seller*

2

1

Musician *Praying man* *Painter*

2

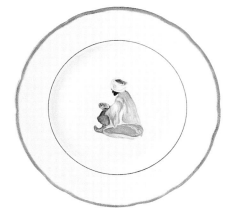
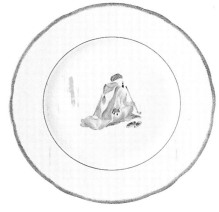

Dessert plate

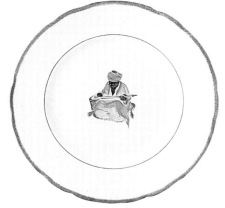

PAINTS

Dessert plate with oriental figures

- The colors used for the motif on the side plate, in addition to the following:
- Smoker: violet blue
- Carpet seller: purple
- Fruit seller: chestnut brown and light wood brown
- Musician: grass green, light wood brown and chocolate brown
- Praying man: border brown
- Painter: golden ruby
- Background and border: Delft blue groundlay

Dessert plate

Proceed as for the side plate but using a richer palette of colors for the clothing and adding a blue border around the center and rim. You will need a banding wheel and cut liner to create the central border. The border around the rim is simply sponged on.

Knife rest

① Paint little palm trees on the upper surface of the knife rest (follow the instructions given for the candlesticks). The piece is now ready for the first firing ①.

② Using masking fluid, resist out the palm trees at both ends of the knife rest. With the make-up brush, dab on brown red groundlay, leave to dry and remove the masking fluid. Fire once again to cure the groundlay.

③ Add shading to the palm trees and sponge Delft blue onto the ends of the knife rest. The piece is now ready for the second firing ②.

Knife rest

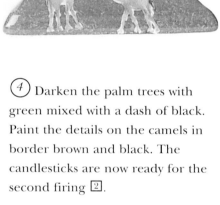

YOU WILL NEED

– Long-haired fine brush
– #4 fitch brush
– Make-up brush (to apply red groundlay)
– Sponge (to apply black groundlay)
– Masking fluid (or resist)
– Masking tape
– Scraper

PAINTS

– Palm trees: grass green, sepia brown, deep brown and brown red ①; chocolate brown and black ②
– Camels: yellow brown, border brown and ivory black
– Backgrounds: brown red and ivory black groundlay

Candlesticks

① Transfer the palm trees and the camels from the drawings on p. 134 onto the candlesticks. Start by painting the trunks of the palm trees sepia brown and deep brown, as a tightly stacked column of little circles. Curve the trunks to make the trees look more natural. Add bold touches of brown red at the top of the trunk to create the dates.

② Next paint the foliage. Start with the curved branches, followed by the fronds on the sides of the branches. Work outwards from the trunk and paint each frond with a single, delicate brushstroke.

③ Paint the camels as for the large plate (see p. 83). Dab with the fitch brush to create a soft finish. The candlesticks are now ready for the first firing ①.

④ Darken the palm trees with green mixed with a dash of black. Paint the details on the camels in border brown and black. The candlesticks are now ready for the second firing ②.

⑤ Mask off the edges of the moldings (with masking tape or fluid) and paint in black groundlay. Fire once again to cure the black groundlay.

⑥ Use masking fluid to resist out the palm trees, camels and black moldings. Now use the make-up brush like a sponge to dab on brown red groundlay over the base and central part of the candlestick. When completely dry, use the scraper to remove the masking fluid. Fire again to cure the groundlay.

LARGE PLATE

The materials are the same as for the side plate

PAINTS

– Palm trees and trees: border brown, grass green, brown red, chocolate brown and ivory black
– Ruins and desert architecture: border brown, sepia brown, chestnut brown, ivory black and chocolate brown
– Sand: sienna
– Figures: sky blue, violet blue, ivory black and sepia
– Camels: light sepia brown, border brown, sky blue, violet blue, ivory black and iron red
– Tents: eye gray, border brown, ivory black, sepia brown and sienna
– Backgrounds and borders: brown red groundlay

Large plate

(1) Carefully transfer the designs from the drawings on p. 133 onto each of the plates. Mix your palette of colors to include as many shades of brown as possible. Paint the design, taking care to keep each part separate: You are aiming to create an overall watercolor effect.

(2) With the fitch brush, lightly stipple the larger painted surfaces (sand, camels and walls) then sharpen any outlines with the rubber tip. It is easier to leave painting the sand until after the first firing. Paint the palm trees

as for the candlesticks. The plate is now ready for the first firing ☐1.

(3) Intensify the color overall, without blurring the different parts of the design: You need the lighter areas to add contrast and translucency. The plate is now ready for the second firing ☐2.

(4) Use the banding wheel to draw the band of color around the center of the plate. With the sponge stipple the border around the rim, making it slightly wider than on the dessert plate. Fire once again to cure the band and the border.

YOU WILL NEED

– Long-haired fine brush
– Masking fluid and scraper
– Make-up brush
– #4 fitch brush
– Pointed metal tip and
  small ruler

PAINTS

– Windows: chestnut brown,
  grass green, brown green,
  yellow red, sepia brown and
  sienna (for the sand)
– Doors: iron red, grass green,
  Meissen green, chestnut
  brown and ivory black
– Backgrounds: brown red,
  sienna and yellow brown
  groundlay

Set of six oriental cups and saucers

_Each of these cups features a large window with a view, a smaller
window displaying an ornament and a closed door (at the back)._

① Carefully trace the windows and doors from the drawings on p. 135. Transfer the open window with a view onto the front of the cup, and the little window onto the side. Transfer the door onto the back of the cup but do not paint until after the first firing, when it will be easier to complete.

The window with a view looks out onto architecture, a woman in a burnoose, tenting and typically oriental trees (olive trees, umbrella pines, banana trees, Cedars of Lebanon and cypress trees). Mix the range of colors as required.

② Paint the leaves of the tree in different shades of green and the trunks in chestnut brown. Paint the roofs of the minarets red, working from the top downwards. Remember to turn the cup so that the brushstroke always comes neatly towards you. Paint the ornament in the little window. Finally, paint a subtle outline around the windows with the fine brush. The cups are now ready for the first firing ①.

③ Paint the doors at the back of the cup in two stages. Start by painting and stippling the door with the fitch brush to obtain a smooth finish. When completely dry, place a little ruler down the middle of the door and holding it firmly in place, score a line along it with a pointed metal tip. You have now created the two halves of the door. Use the scraper to add more decorative lines. The cups are now ready for the second firing ②.

④ Darken the outlines, doors and windows of the minarets in black. Darken the leaves on the trees with touches of green mixed with a dash of black. Shade along one side of the trees in chestnut brown. Add touches of color to the ornaments in the windows (earthenware jars, knife, pipe, oriental slippers), shading them in places but leaving lighter areas to create contrast and translucency.

⑤ Complete the doors with ivory black, Meissen green for the geometric paneling and so forth. Fire for the third time ③.

⑥ Resist out the handle, windows and doors with masking fluid. Resist out the center of the saucer then use the make-up brush to apply matching groundlay to the cup and saucer; you are aiming for a background with a granite-like finish.

Leave to dry and remove the resist with a scraper. Fire once again to cure the groundlay.

1   2   3   1   2

1   2   1   2   3

1   2   3   1   2

Practical
tips

USING COLOR

MATERIALS

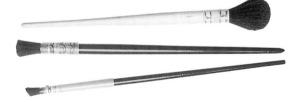

TECHNIQUES

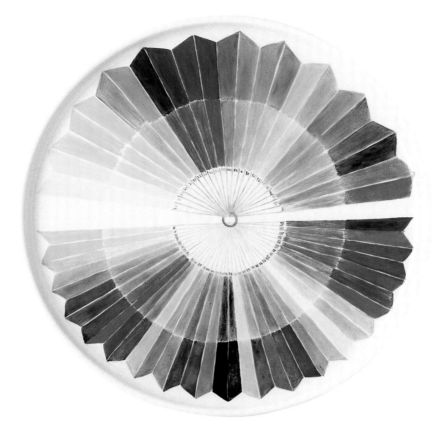

USING COLOR

The colors

The range and palettes of colors shown here represent a real basis from which to work. The colors at the top of the fan are more intense than the paler, more muted colors in the center. In the past, porcelain painters painted a wide range of very useful as well as highly decorative objects and learned what to expect of a color after firing. Some of these objects are now collectors' items in famous museums.

Firing has a significant effect on the intensity of the final tone, so to avoid any unwelcome surprises it is worth assembling your own palette of colors. You can also experiment by mixing your own colors, noting the precise amounts of each color used to create different shades and tints (for example, 3/4 spring green plus 1/4 ivory black). If you are a beginner, start with a basic palette of about 10 colors; two blues (one light, one dark), two yellows, two greens, one gray, one brown, one black and one white. Be careful to use only lead-free on-glaze paints.

Alternatively, buy a beginner's kit containing a set of basic paints and useful accessories.

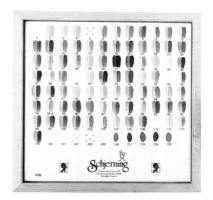

Mix your own colors using black to create darker shades and white to create lighter tints. Gradually add new colors and mixes to the palette and fire as often as you need to.

Record the colors you use in a notebook – do not rely on memory, particularly as you become more adventurous and start to expand your palette. Providing you note each color down, you can return to an unfinished piece several months later and know exactly which color to use.

Firing porcelain paints

Porcelain paints are usually fired in a special porcelain oven at temperatures of 1470-1580°F (800-860°C). For best results with products and ovens, always follow the manufacturer's instructions.

Paints containing cadmium – a delicate white metal found in some reds and oranges – should not be fired at temperatures higher than 1435°F (780°C) as there is a risk that they might burn and develop grayish streaks. You might even lose the color altogether. Many reds, on the other hand, can safely be fired at 1470°F (800°C). Blues should be fired at 1562-1580°F (850-860°C) to keep them shiny (alternatively, add a small amount of flux). Purples and carmines tolerate temperatures of 1508-1544°F (820-840°C). Yellows remain shiny at 1470°F (800°C), but can become discolored when mixed. Take care to find out which of the yellows in your range are suitable for mixing.

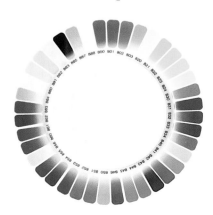

Flux

Paints are composed of metal oxides and flux. It is this flux that allows the paint to fuse with the glaze on the porcelain, ensuring that the color stays shiny when fired at a certain temperature. However, some paints, when applied thinly and fired at normal temperatures, are not shiny enough. To keep them bright, add a small amount of flux and fire at a higher temperature (blue groundlay in particular should be mixed with flux and fired at 1580°F (860°C)). Be careful because flux has a lightening effect.

Groundlay

Groundlay is paint used to create colored backgrounds. It is mixed with groundlay oil (thick fat oil), applied evenly with a broad, flat brush and finally dabbed quickly with a sponge pad (see 'Mixing Groundlay', p. 94).

Gold and platinum

These are precious metals in liquid form. Gold may be bright or mat and generally contains 24-30 percent gold (never buy paints containing less than

this). Platinum may also be bright or mat. All precious metals should be stirred for several minutes with an orange stick to prevent the formation of black streaks after firing. If you think the paint is too thick, add a drop of thinner and mix well. Use a separate brush for each metal and clean with thinner.

Usually, gold and platinum are added last of all onto white porcelain. So remember to use masking tape or fluid to mask off any areas that are to remain white. Gold and platinum should be fired at 1470°F (800°C) when applied to white porcelain. If applied to colored backgrounds, they should be fired at 1202°F (650°C) to avoid cracks forming in the metal paint. Mat gold and platinum are black on application and should be applied in thick, smooth layers. They should be polished after firing with a burnishing pad or burnishing sand. Bright gold and platinum should be applied smoothly and thinly – never thickly. They should be light brown in color to ensure a good 'reflective' effect after firing. They do not need polishing.

MATERIALS

The following list includes a brief description of the brushes, products and materials used to create the pieces in this book. The items listed are suggestions only. Specialist shops stock a range of brushes and mixing products that would do just as well. For the best results, follow manufacturers' instructions.

Brushes
Clean your brushes with orange oil or turpentine, followed by soapy water. To keep them in good condition, dip in oil and store in a vertical position, tip uppermost.

Long-haired fine brush (1): the classic brush for painting small motifs.
– Use squirrel (or sable) pointer brush #0 or #1 (see illustration).

Long-haired medium brush (2): the classic brush for painting larger motifs.
– Use squirrel (or sable) pointer brush #4 (see illustration)

Fitch brush (3): rounded, beveled, deerfoot stippling brush.
– Use to create an even finish and to stipple the color where required after application with a fine or medium-point brush (see illustration).

Cut liner: long-haired brush, cut at an angle.
– Use to paint lines when using the banding wheel.

Make-up brush (4):
– Use to create speckled backgrounds with a granite-like or sandy finish, and to stipple paint onto surfaces. (see illustration).

Pointer brush for masking fluid (5): short, fine-point brush and short, medium-point brush.
– Use cheap pointers and paintbrushes that you no longer use for other paints (see illustration). Clean with soapy water after use.

Brush to apply gold and platinum (6): short fine-point brush and short, medium-point brush.
– Use squirrel or sable pointer No 2 and paintbrushes that you no longer use for other paints (see illustration).

Long liner (7): very long-tipped brush to apply a line or band of color to pieces on the banding wheel.
– Use squirrel or sable pointer (see illustration).

Broad, flat brush (8):
– Use to spread groundlay before dabbing with the sponge. Usually available in squirrel only (see illustration).

Oils and other materials

Adhesive tape: Use to mark off edges.
Denatured alcohol: Use to degrease and remove dirt from porcelain objects.
General purpose medium and fat oil:
– General purpose medium comes ready-mixed for use with powder paints. It can be thinned with turpentine or orange oil.
– Fat oil can also be mixed with powder paints. It is important to use the oil in the correct proportions so as to obtain a thick mixture (unlike the medium) and to thin it with turpentine, orange oil or oil of aspic (labiatae), cloves or lavender.

Both general purpose medium and fat oil are equally good. The choice is yours.

Lavender or clove oil: Use essences to dilute colors and

delay drying. When painting large areas of groundlay, add a drop of lavender or clove essences, general purpose medium or fat oil.

Masking fluid: Thick, red liquid used to mask off areas. Scrape off with a metallic tip before firing and remove with fine tweezers. After use, clean your brush with soapy water.

Orange oil: Use to clean your brushes and as a substitute thinner to turpentine.

Pen oil: Aqueous medium for mixing colors to be applied by pen.

Thinner for gold and platinum: Use to thin precious metals in liquid form; clean your brush as before.

Turpentine: Use to thin colors and clean brushes.

Other useful materials

In addition to the list above, the following items may also prove useful. Once again, however, the list is not exhaustive. More tools and products are available from specialist shops.

Banding wheel: Small turntable to help you paint lines with a long-haired brush.

Burnishing pad: Glass fiber instrument for polishing mat gold and platinum paints. You can also use burnishing sand.

Ceramic mixing tile: Use as a base for mixing powder paints and as a palette.

Chinagraph or Stabilo pencil: Use to draw directly onto porcelain; marks disappear on firing.

Cotton swabs: You will need plenty of these for retouching and cleaning. Dip the cotton swab in methylated spirit, wiping off any excess with a cloth, then wipe neatly around the piece to be decorated. Use a damp cotton swab for retouching (to erase or correct mistakes).

Gold eraser: Use to rub off unwanted fired gold.

Graphite and tracing paper: Use to transfer a design: place the tracing paper face down on the piece to be decorated and tape the tracing over it.

Lining tool: Metal instrument to create circles around an edge.

Mapping pen: Use to draw motifs using aqueous medium or pen-oil.

Orange stick: To mix paints on the ceramic tile, stir gold and platinum, etc.

Palette knife with supple blade: To mix powder paint and essences.

Palette box: To store paints away from dust and air for several days.

Plastic spatula: Use to mix gold and platinum.

Porcelain oven: If you have a high output of work, you might find it more convenient to buy your own porcelain oven. These are available as small capacity ovens that run off a domestic electricity supply. Programs can be pre-recorded but do bear in mind that different colors are fired at different temperatures (see 'Firing porcelain paints,' p. 90). Also check the safety regulations.

Rubber tip (or color shaper): Very useful for retouching designs before the paint dries.

Scraper: Essential for retouching designs once the paint has dried.

Sponge pad: You need these in all shapes and sizes to apply groundlay (background color). When used to apply paints mixed with turpentine, clean after use with turpentine. When used to apply paints mixed with fat oil and thinning essence, clean after use with methylated spirit. Then clean with soapy water and leave to dry before re-use.

Sponge roller: Cut out a piece of sponge and tape onto a sponge pad. Use to create groundlay with a very fine-grained finish.

Stylus: Pressing quite firmly, go over the tracing with a hard-tipped instrument.

TECHNIQUES

Transferring the designs

Use graphite paper to transfer a design from this book onto the ceramic surface. Trace the design onto a blank sheet of paper. First tape the graphite paper onto the ceramic piece and then your traced drawing over it. Using a stylus, trace over the design so that the image rubs off on the ceramic.

Mixing the paints

First clean a ceramic tile with alcohol. Next, use the point of a knife to place a small amount of powder paint on the tile. Add general purpose medium and mix well with a palette knife to obtain a smooth mixture. If using fat oil, dip the knife in the bottle of oil so as to remove no more than is necessary and mix with the powder paint. Adjust the mix to the consistency required, using the appropriate essences.

Mixing paints to apply by brush

– With general purpose medium.
  For intense color, add very
  little medium. For more muted
  effects, add slightly more. You
  may find that as you work, the
  paint thickens, in which case
  add a few drops of turpentine
  (or orange oil) and mix well.
– With fat oil.
  It is important to use the
  correct proportion of fat oil to
  paint so as to obtain a thick
  consistency and avoid the risk

of the color breaking up during firing. Thinner is added last of all. It is the thinner that changes the depth of color, not the fat oil. For intense color, add a few drops of thinner (turpentine, orange oil, oil of aspic or cloves). For a more muted effect, add a bit more.

Mixing groundlay

Mix the paints as for those applied by brush (either method) using the palette knife to crush each grain of color (this may take a few minutes). If necessary, to keep the color bright after firing, add a dash of flux on the point of a knife. Groundlay needs to be more liquid than paint applied by brush so add a drop of oil of cloves. Apply the groundlay with a broad, flat brush then dab all over quickly with the sponge pad.

Mixing color for pen work and outlining

Pen work can be useful to draw particularly complicated motifs (architectural designs, people, repeat patterns, etc). Dissolve half a sugar cube in a few drops of water. On a mixing tile, mix a small amount of this solution with the powder paint until you obtain a relatively thin liquid suitable for pen work (you can also mix the powder paint with ready-mixed pen oil). Then draw the decoration with this mixture.

It will dry quickly, even without firing, and remain in place during subsequent brushwork. Once you have learned to handle a brush with confidence, you will resort to the pen less and less.

Basic brushwork techniques

Filling the brush

Having mixed your paints on the ceramic tile and chosen your brushes, open your brush as you stroke it through the paint. Then restore its natural pointed shape by wiping off any excess on a clean part of the tile. You have now filled your brush with the right amount of paint.

Painting

Always draw the brush down and toward you. This is essential to give you control over each brushstroke. Rotate the piece you are painting to ensure this downward brushstroke – even if it means painting part of the motif upside down! Start by applying the paint thinly; you want to create translucency and contrast. You can always darken a motif after firing, but you can never take color away. Add areas of light and shade afterward.

Cleaning and correcting

Once you have finished painting the basic motifs, wipe around them neatly. Use a rubber tip (or color shaper) to perfect or

Figure 1

Figure 2

Figure 3

Figure 4

Figure 5

retouch an outline, or damp cotton swabs to correct or erase part of the drawing. Use cotton swabs dipped in denatured alcohol to clean stains around the motifs and at the back of the object. Once the paint has dried, you can always use a scraper to make corrections. After the first firing, this white background provides the basis for the effects you want to create.

Creating contrast and texture

There are various ways in which to make a motif stand out against a white background. These include shading, rounding off, emphasizing creases in leaves and folds in clothing, highlighting the silkiness of petals and toning down areas that are too light. Create the motifs first and add groundlay, edging and lines afterwards to 'trim' and enhance your designs.

This leaves you free to modify, and in many cases, improve the basic motifs as you work. By creating backgrounds and

lines around your motifs, rather than vice versa, you will be taking a major step toward a more personal style.

A step-by-step guide to painting leaves on trees

Painting leaves on trees, whatever the species, is always a pleasure. The following four-step guide contains tips on how to create all sorts of leaves – wavy, large and small – using just a few brushstrokes. Of course, you can apply the same basic principles to create any of the decorations featured in this book.

Basic technique

Complete each side of the leaf separately, starting in the middle each time and working downwards. Begin by placing the tip of the brush on the surface, then push it down with a curve (figure 1) and lift off to create a curved tip. Repeat beneath for the next curve and continue until you have a

complete set of curves, right and left. Then trace a central spine from top to bottom as a single, fine, free-flowing curved stroke (figure 2). You now have a leaf shape (figure 3). Turn it upside down and use the rubber tip to create a serrated edge: working downwards, make little notches along the edge of the leaf (figure 4). Clean and fire.

Darken part of the leaf and shade half or three quarters of it with more intense color. Use the same technique to create a lighter area (figure 5). The same principles may be applied to create other leaf shapes.

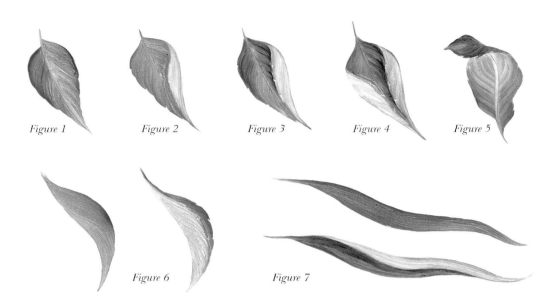

Figure 1   *Figure 2*   *Figure 3*   *Figure 4*   *Figure 5*

Figure 6   *Figure 7*

Creating movement

With just a few brushstrokes, you can make your leaf look wavy or twisted and introduce an infinite range of movement. After painting the leaf (figure 1), rinse your brush in orange oil and dry with a (lint free) cloth. Then apply color over the small area that you want to twist in the opposite direction to the rest of the leaf (figure 2). Clean and restore the outline if necessary using a moistened cotton swab. After firing, darken the inside of the leaf under the fold for greater suppleness (figure 3).

Apply the same technique to fold over both sides of a leaf (figure 4), the tip (figure 5) or to fold it in half completely (figures 6 and 7).

Mastering these basic brushstrokes is as useful as it is fun. Practice as often as you need to on a ceramic tile.

The art of overlay

To make a motif look more realistic and more natural, you can overlay part of the leaf on another (figure 8). Proceed as if the first leaf did not exist and paint part of the second leaf over it. Give the new leaf a different direction and movement and use a slightly lighter color. Place the tip of the brush on the surface, press down and bring back to a point several times. Do this until you have entirely covered the lines of the leaf beneath. For best results, use several thin layers of fresh paint that will not dilute each other. Use the rubber tip to create a discreet delineation between the two leaves and the leaves and berries.

Once dry, use a scraper to slim down the stems, round off the berries and add movement to the leaves. Fire, then darken branches, along the insides of folds on leaves and along the edges where leaves and berries meet or are overlaid.

A world of shapes

This basic technique, embellished by movement and overlay, is all you need to create a virtually infinite range of shapes and forms.

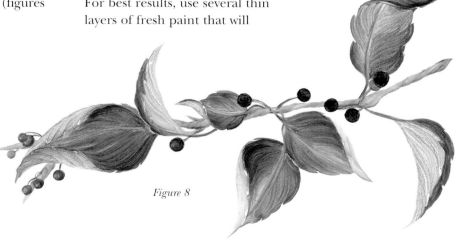

Figure 8

BONBONS AND CANDY CANES

NAUGHTY IMPS

Soup dish

Tumbler

Eggcup

APPLES, CATERPILLARS AND SEEDS

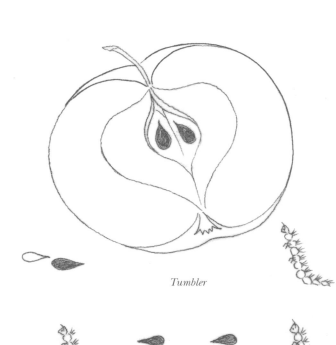

Tumbler

Soup dish

Eggcup

Soup dish

Tumbler

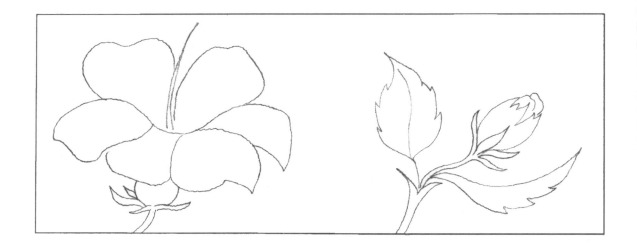

Hibiscus cup

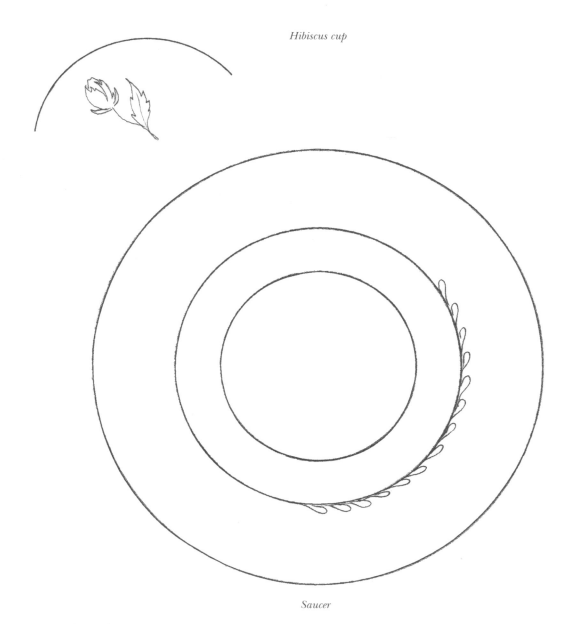

Saucer

Pansy cup

Magnolia cup

Tulip cup

Dandelion cup

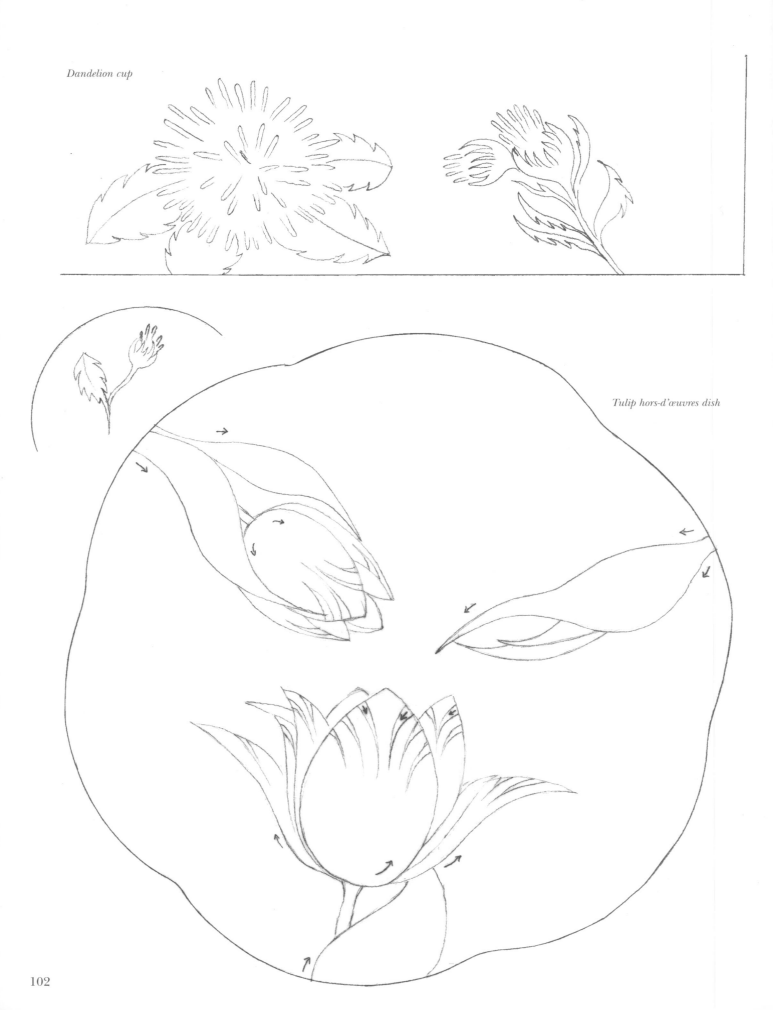

Tulip hors-d'œuvres dish

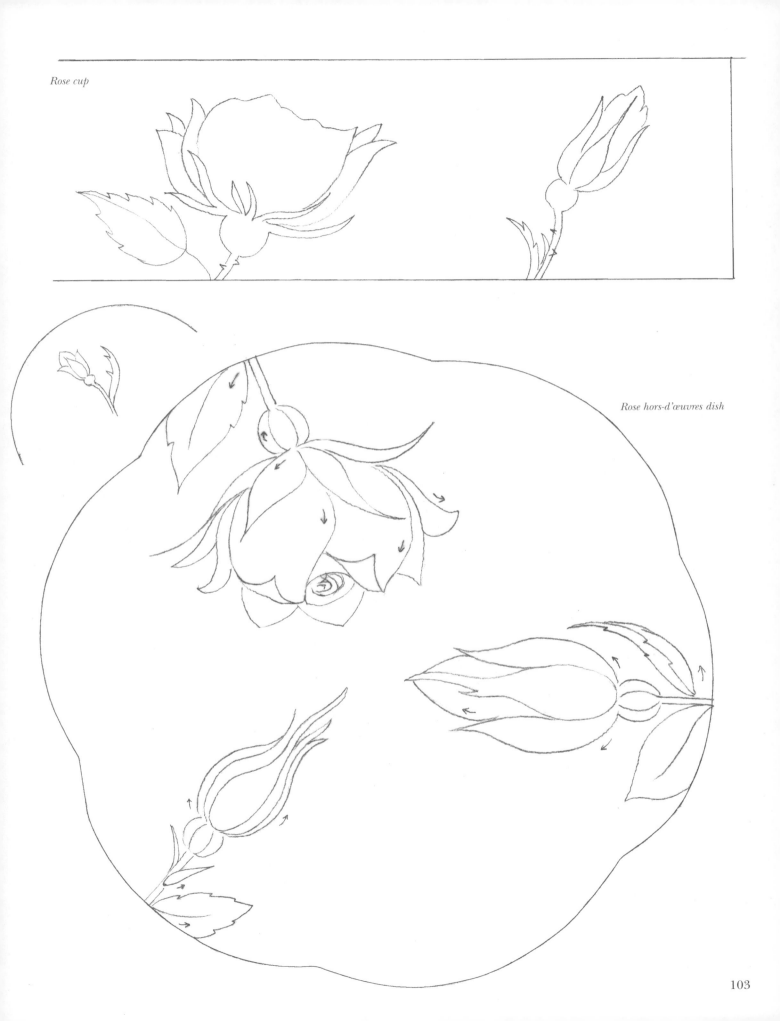

Rose cup

Rose hors-d'œuvres dish

Pearl gray cup

Rich blue cup

Yellow red cup

Albert Yellow cup

Yellow green saucer

Purple saucer

Albert yellow saucer

Pearl gray saucer

Rich blue saucer

Yellow red saucer

Purple cup

Yellow green cup

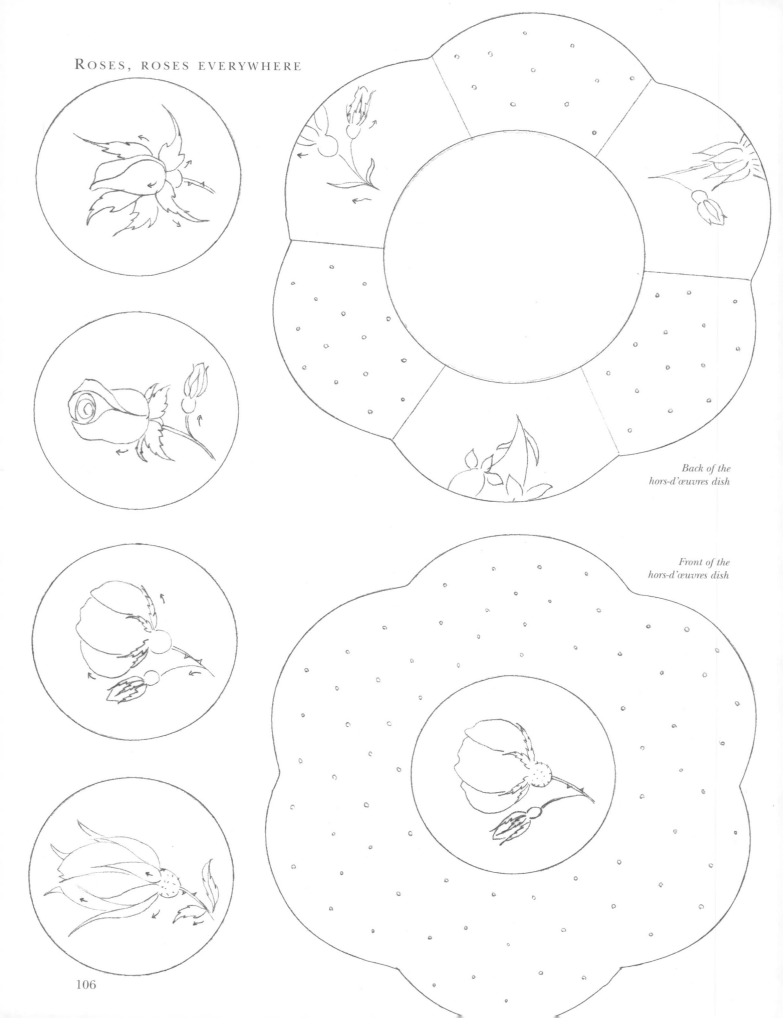

Back of the hors-d'œuvres dish

Front of the hors-d'œuvres dish

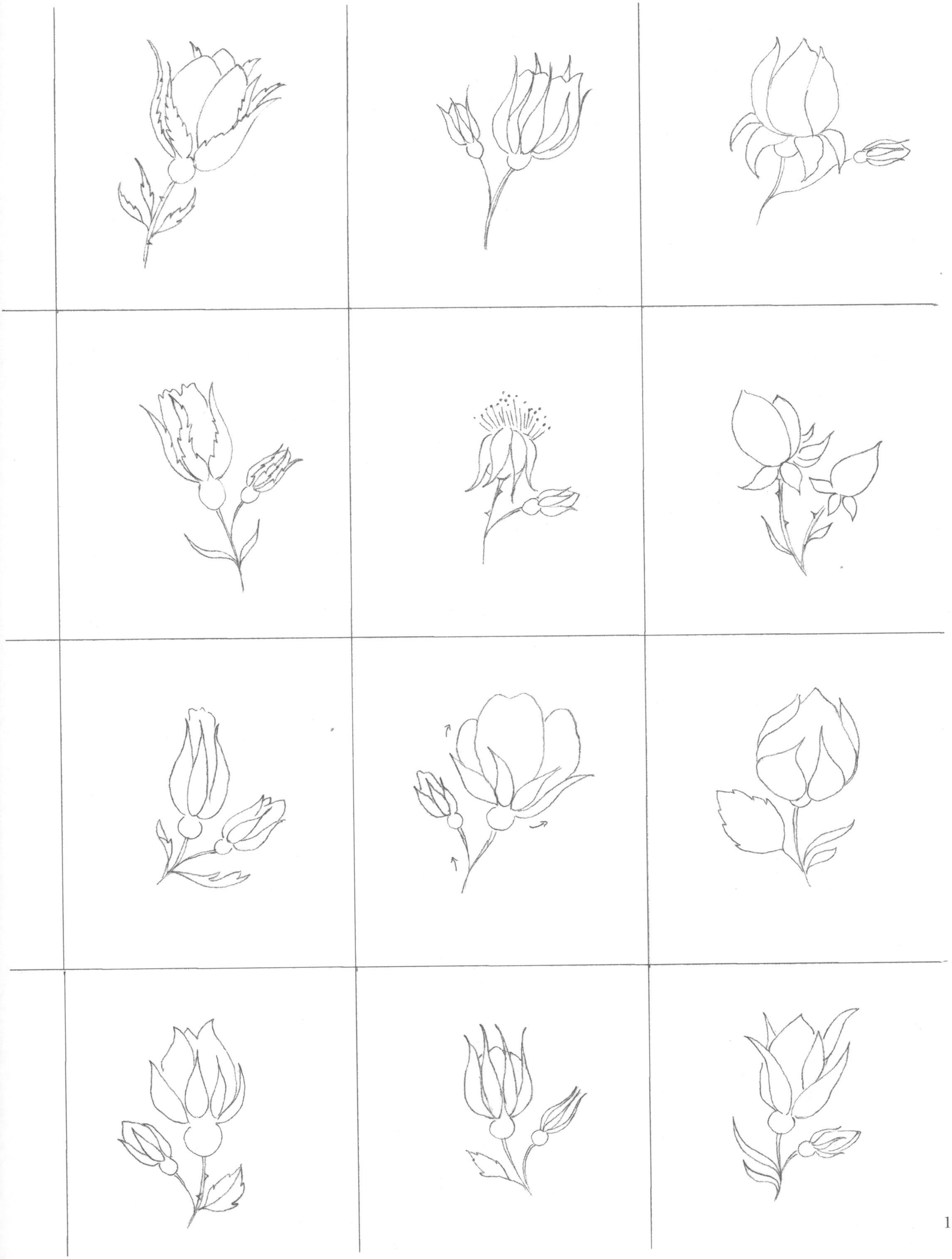

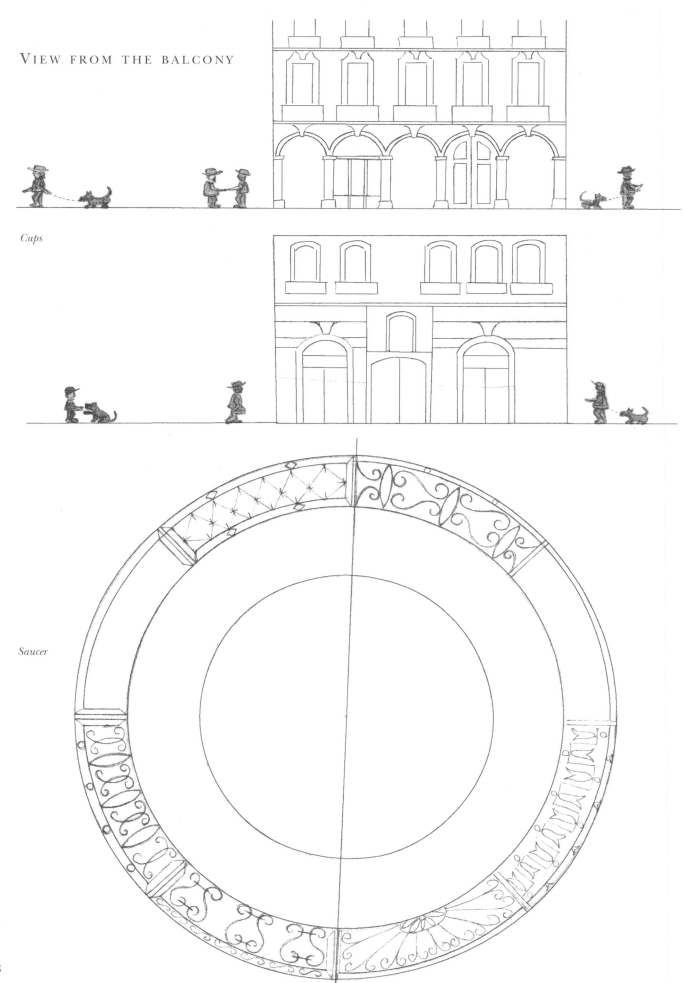

VIEW FROM THE BALCONY

Cups

Saucer

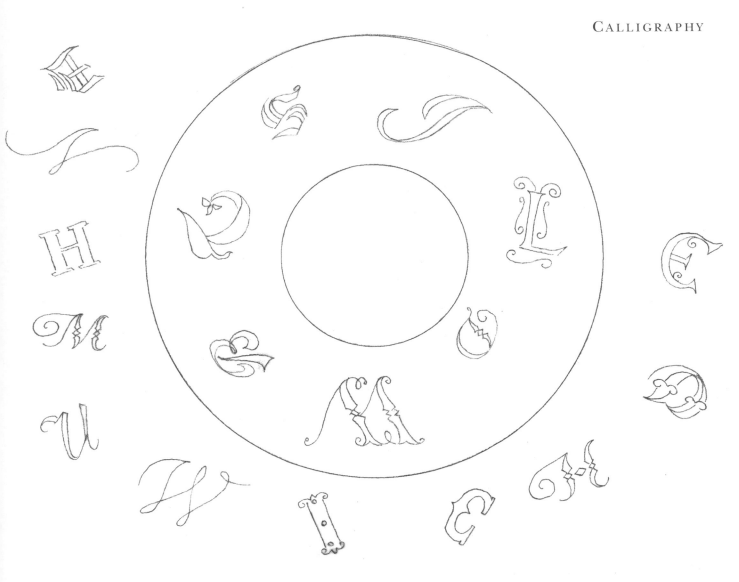

Saucer

Cup

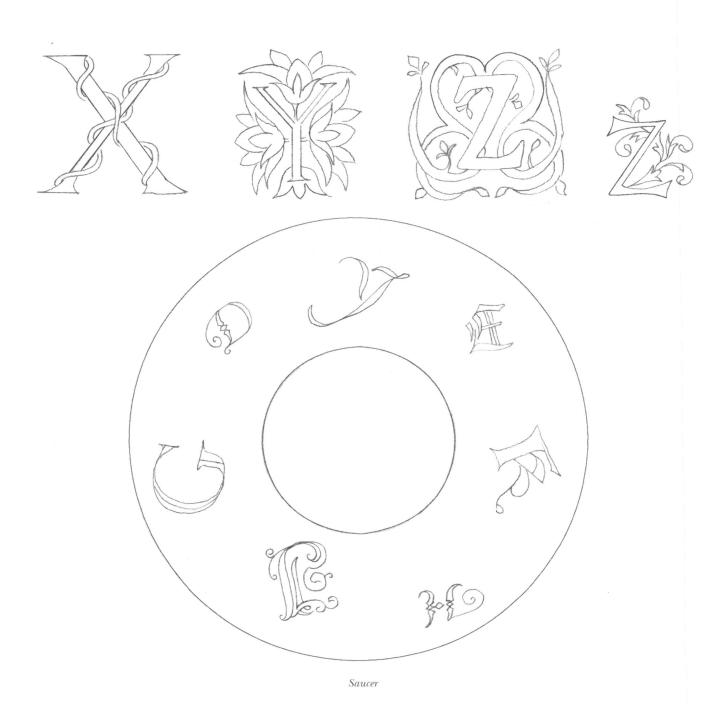

Saucer

Cup

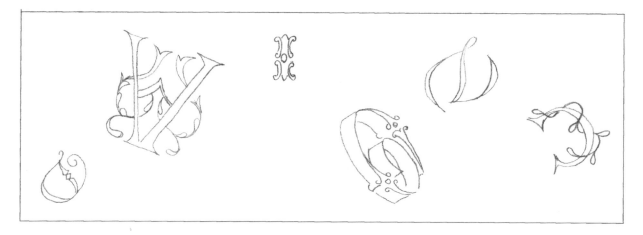

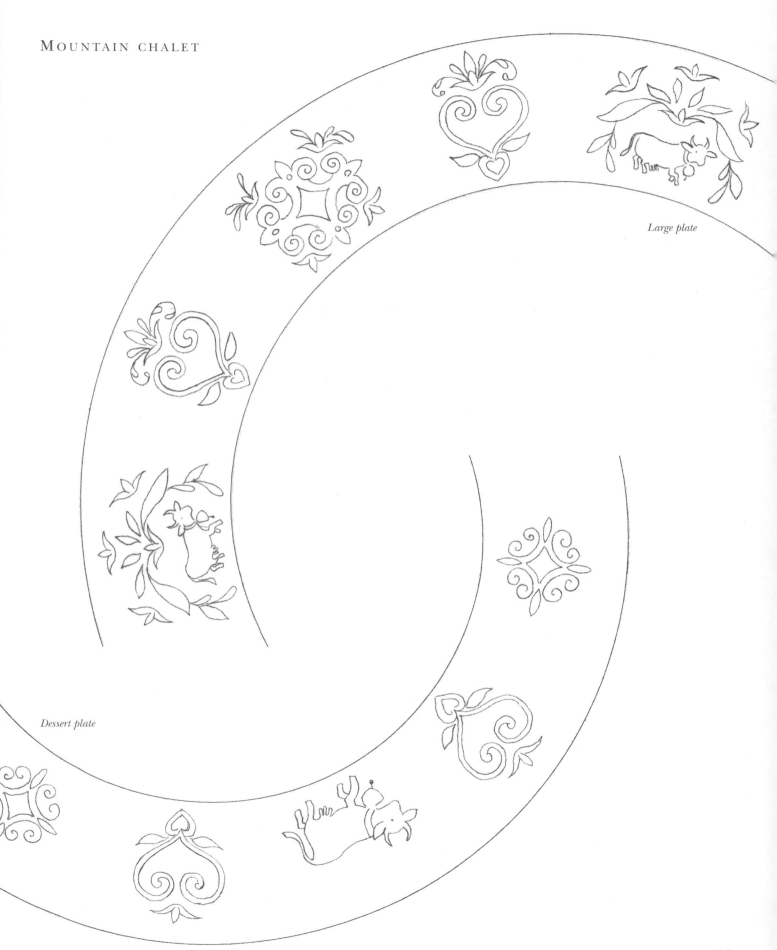

Large plate

Dessert plate

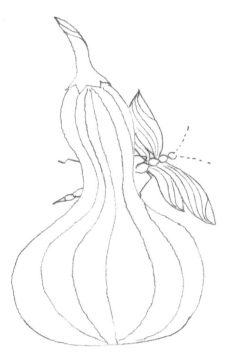

Dish with butternut squash

Dish with pumpkin squash

Dish with green squash

Dish with white squash

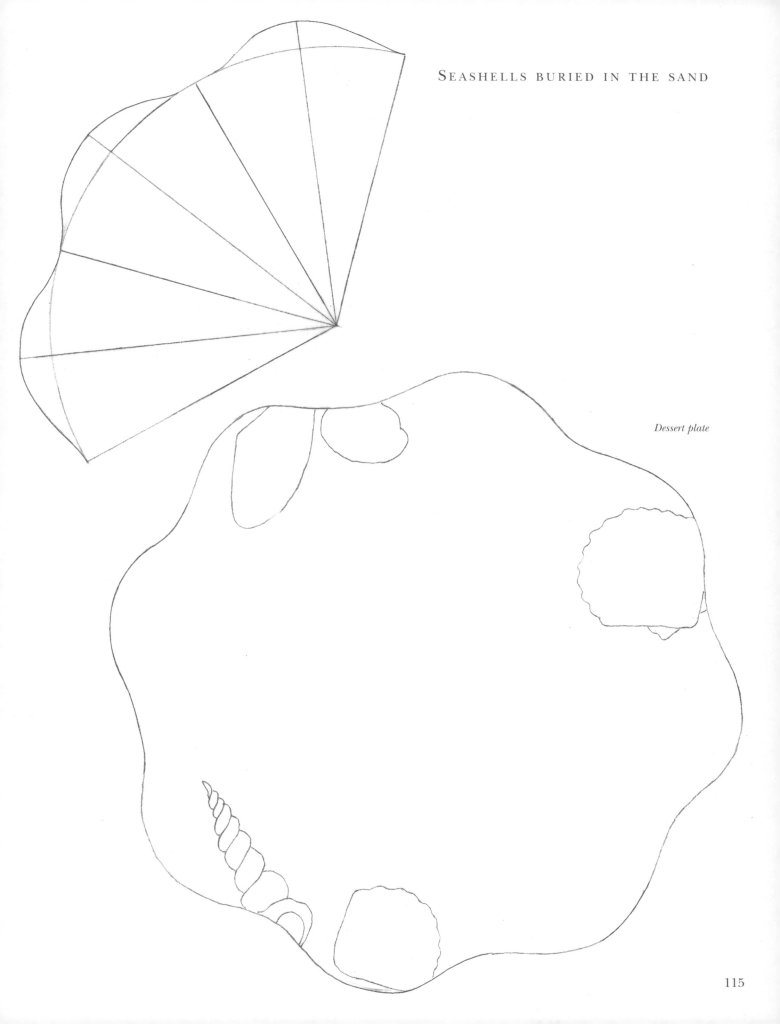

Dessert plate

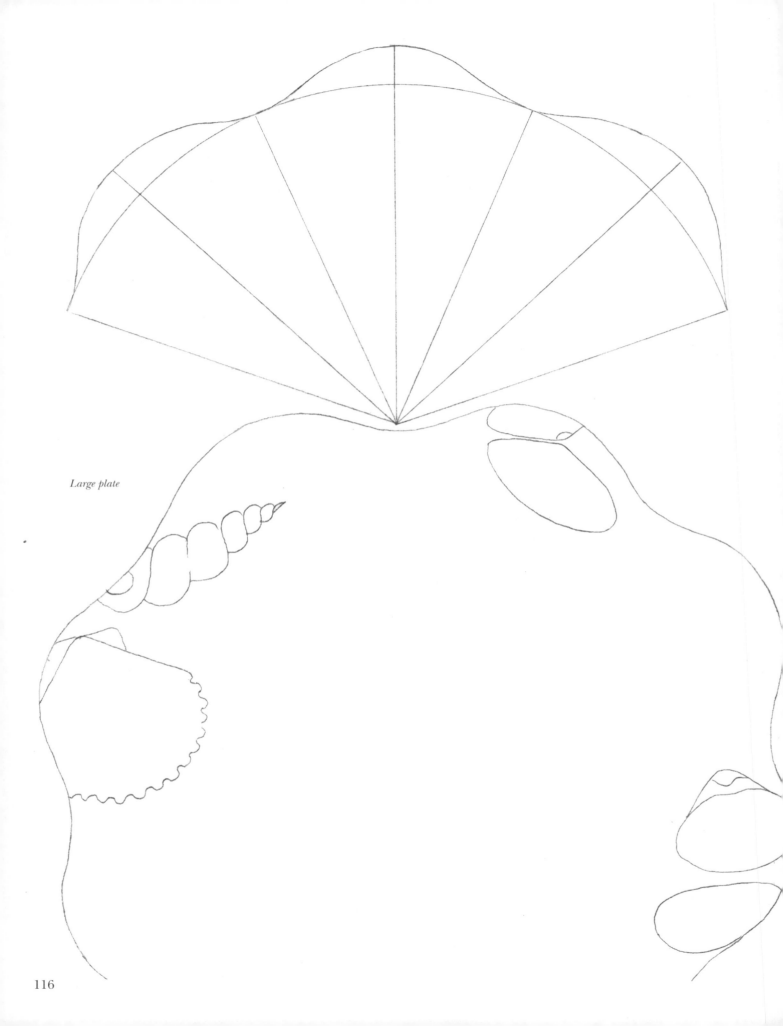

Large plate

Large plate with mimosa border

Side plate with garland of mimosa

Dessert plate with bouquet of mimosa

Large plate with pansy border

Side plate with garland of pansy

Dessert plate with bouquet of pansies

Large plate with sunflower border   Side plate with garland of sunflowers

Dessert plate with bouquet of sunflowers

Large plate with rose border

Side plate with garland of roses

Dessert plate with bouquet of roses

Large plate with tulip border   *Side plate with garland of tulips*

Dessert plate with bouquet of tulips

Large plate with broom border

Side plate with garland of broom

Dessert plate with bouquet of broom

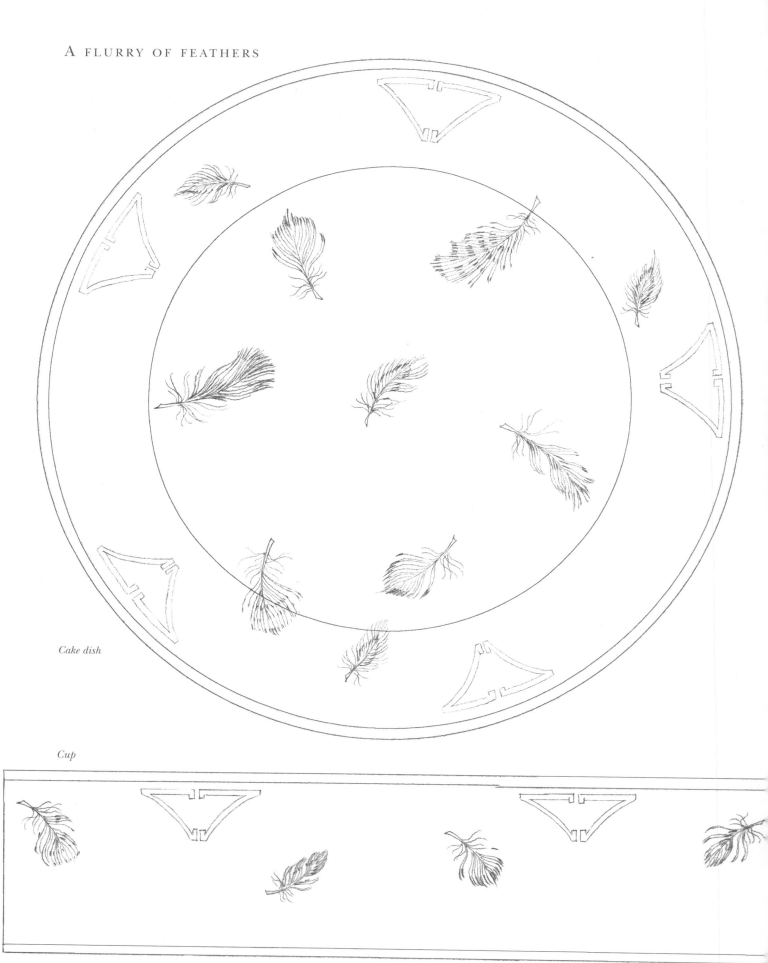

Cake dish

Cup

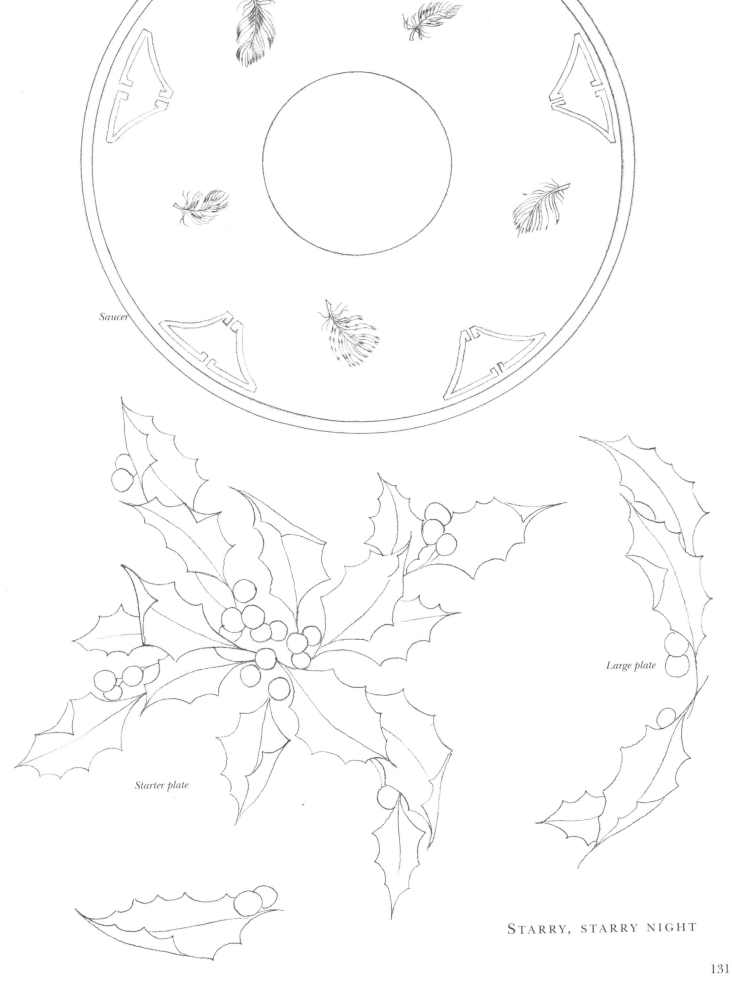

Saucer

Large plate

Starter plate

STARRY, STARRY NIGHT

Side plates and dessert plates

Candlestick

Knife rest

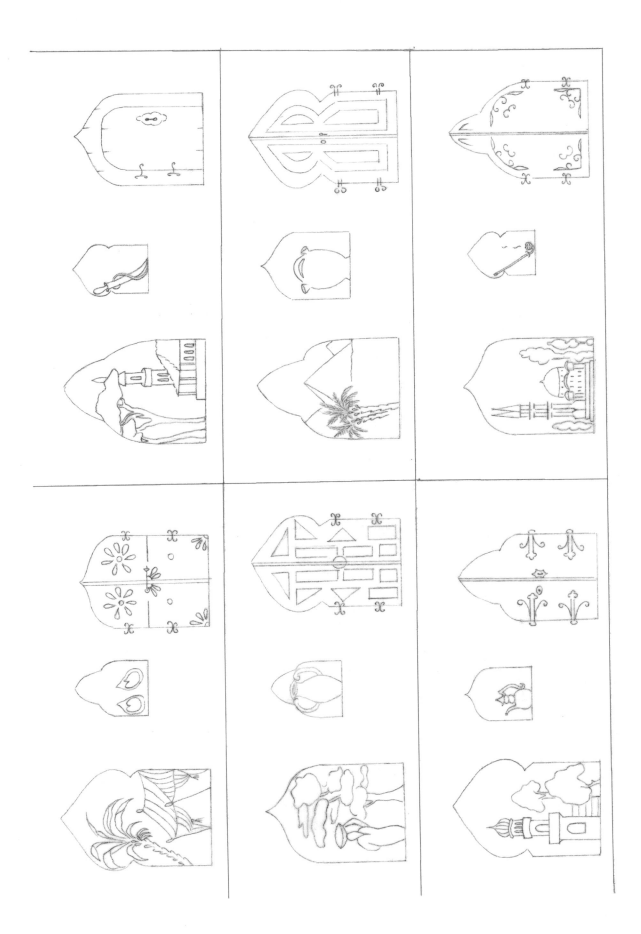

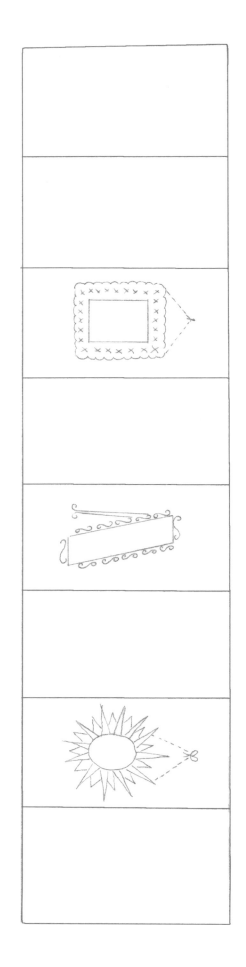

INDEX